The *Jesus Family Tomb* Controversy:

How the evidence falls short

By Dillon Burroughs

NIMBLE BOOKS LLC

NIMBLE BOOKS LLC

ISBN 978-0-9788138-7-1

Copyright 2007 Dillon Burroughs

Last saved 2007-03-19.

Nimble Books LLC

1521 Martha Avenue

Ann Arbor, MI 48103-5333

http://www.nimblebooks.com

Other Works by Dillon Burroughs

Comparing Christianity with World Religions (with Steven Cory), Chicago, IL: Moody, 2007.

Comparing Christianity with the Cults (with Keith Brooks and Irvine Robertson), Chicago, IL: Moody, 2007.

Get in the Game (with Tony Evans and Jonathan Evans), Chicago, IL: Moody, 2006.

Middle East Meltdown coauthored with John Ankerberg, Eugene, OR: Harvest House, 2007.

Misquotes in Misquoting Jesus, Ann Arbor, MI: Nimble Books, 2006.

The Use of the Bible in The Da Vinci Code, Amazon, 2006.

The Da Vinci Code Controversy (with Michael Easley and John Ankerberg), Chicago, IL: Moody, 2006.

What's the Big Deal About Jesus? (coauthored with John Ankerberg), Eugene, OR: Harvest House, available August 2007.

Nimble Books LLC

Contents

Other Works by Dillon Burroughs iii

Contents iv

Acknowledgements vii

Introduction: A Skeleton in God's Closet? 1

    Dillon's Story 6

It's All in the Names: Are These Names Really So Special? 9

    Jesus son of Joseph 11

    Maria 12

    Jose 13

    Judah son of Jesus 13

    Mariamene e Mara 15

    Matia (or Matya) 17

Multilingual Madness: Why Are There Three Languages in One Tomb? ... 20

    What Languages Are Included? 20

    Additional Scenarios 22

        Option 1: Each language refers to a different family 22

        Option 2: The Multiple Languages Involve a Multilingual Family .. 23

        Option 3: The Tomb Was Designed for Those with the Ability to Afford It 23

        Option 4: The Tomb Inscriptions Were Forged 24

        Option 5: The Different Languages Are Due to Different Generations 24

Hometown Heroes: Wasn't Jesus from Nazareth? 26

    Nazareth in History 27

    Nazareth in the New Testament..27

    Nazareth in the Tomb Special 29

There's DNA! It Must Be True... What Does the DNA Test Prove? 32

Mary, Mary, Quite Contrary: How Can We Tell Mary Is Mary Magdalene? 38

        That she was a follower of Jesus...39

        That she was married to Jesus and had a child named Jude............ 42

        That She is the Mary Ossuary in the Talpiot Tomb. 48

    Where Does the Evidence Lead Regarding the So-Called Mary Magdalene Ossuary?...51

Who Was the Beloved Disciple? 53

    At the Last Supper 54

    In the Garden 55

    At the Cross..58

    Is Judah the Beloved Disciple?...60

    Was Thomas the Twin the Beloved Disciple? 60

    Who Was the Beloved Disciple?..62

    Evidence of Apostle John's Authorship of the Gospel of John 64

Revising Christian Theology: What Would It Really Change?.....................67

Stats About Stats: How Did They Come Up with Their Statistics?...............77

O Brother, Where Art Thou? What About the Controversial James Ossuary?.. 86

Parting Words: How to Handle The Jesus Family Tomb 92

    Mistakes to Avoid 93

    What Should We Say about The Lost Tomb of Jesus? 98

Appendix A: Additional Quotes Regarding *The Family Tomb of Jesus* 102

Appendix B: Nine Facts That Disapprove the Discovery Channel's The Lost Tomb of Jesus 105

Appendix C: Would The Followers of Jesus Have Taken His Body? 114

    Asking the Tough Questions 115

    Questioning the Disciples Concerning the Empty Tomb 115

        Did They Have A Motive? 115

        Did They Have A Plan? 116

        Did They Have the Resources? 117

        Did They Have the Connections? 119

About the Author 137

Publisher Information 139

    Amazon Upgrade 139

    Ordering This Book in Quantity 139

    About Nimble Books 139

Colophon 140

Acknowledgements

I would like to personally thank those thinkers and scholars whose writings and research have greatly enhanced the making of this book. These include Dr. John Ankerberg. Dr. Ben Witherington, Dr. Daniel Wallace, Dr. Darrell Bock, Dr. Craig Evans and Dr. Gary Habermas.

My deepest thanks to Fred Zimmerman, my partner on this project at Nimble Books. His vision, positive feedback, and hard work are what made this book physically possible.

Deep gratitude is expressed to the Ankerberg Theological Research Institute staff, including Alan Weathers, Beth Lamberson, Darlene Ankerberg, Michelle Ankerberg, Ruth, Ben, Jack, and the rest of the team. I'm looking forward to our continued ministry together. I also appreciate the use of some of the articles and other research we have used in other contexts that have influenced my thinking on this issue.

My personal appreciation extends to Mark Tobey, a good friend, brother, and former editor of Moody Publishing. He has been the one person most influential in encouraging my early publishing.

Trevor Elliott, my technology expert and one of my best friends has been an essential part of this and other books. Thanks, Trevor, for your tremendous efforts behind the scenes.

A special thanks to my best friend and wife, Deborah, for listening to my ideas, putting up with my early mornings of writing at Starbucks, and for standing beside me through every moment of the process. I love you! To my kids, Ben and Natalie, I love you so much! Thanks for making Daddy's life so special!

Lastly, my thanks to Jesus Christ, the one who fuels my faith and writing. May he be honored through these words.

Introduction: A Skeleton in God's Closet?

An ancient skeleton is discovered in Israel.

Will it shed light on the life of Jesus

Or plunge the world into darkness and chaos?

These words are found on the back of the 1994 bestselling Christian novel by Dr. Paul Maier called *A Skeleton in God's Closet*.[1] In it, Dr. Jonathan Weber, a Harvard professor and biblical scholar, joins an archaeological dig in Israel that seems to hold the very bones of Jesus of Nazareth. Entertaining and inspiring, the story concluded with Dr. Weber's discovery of the find's forgery, helping to restore the faith of millions of Christians worldwide who had lost hope at the thought someone finding the body of Jesus.

Fast forward 13 years later to February 26, 2007. At a major press conference, filmmakers and researchers unveiled two ancient stone boxes they claim may have once contained the remains of Jesus and Mary Magdalene—*except this time it's not fiction*. On Sunday, March 4, 2007, "The Lost Tomb of Jesus," produced by Oscar-winning director James Cameron aired nationwide on the Discovery Channel. A related book by Simcha and Charles Pellegrino entitled *The Jesus Family Tomb: The Discovery, the Investigation, and the Evidence That Could Change History*[2] released the day of the press conference to coordinate with the special. Further, the special was not only aired worldwide, but rather in Canada (via the Vision network) and in Europe (via C-4 and other networks).

These researchers argue that 10 small caskets discovered in 1980 in a Jerusalem suburb may have held the bones of Jesus and his family. They even claim that one of the caskets bears the title, "Judah, son of Jesus," hinting that Jesus may have had a son. But what truth can be found in this story?

The truth is that several unsupportable assumptions have been made to provide maximum hype for the book and television event. According to an interview with Dallas Seminary professor Dr. Darrell Bock in the *Dallas Observer*, "They are claiming as fact assumptions that they are making. And those assumptions all have to line up for it to be true."[3]

How was this tomb discovered? Israeli archaeologist Professor Amos Kloner was the first to find the tomb in 1980. He found the tomb and the ossuaries—the urns or vaults used to hold the bones of the dead—interesting, but of no particular archaeological importance. He says there are more than 900 buried tombs just like the "Jesus" tomb within a two-mile radius of Talpiot. Of them, 71 bear the name Jesus and two use Jesus, son of Joseph. The tomb in Talpiot is one of them. But the inscription, he says, was barely decipherable and therefore questionable.

At the time, Jesus was a very common name, as was Mary. But the cluster of all those names together, Jesus, Joseph, Mary, not to mention what the filmmakers claim is Jesus' son, "Judah, son of Jesus," is somewhat unusual. But simply because the tomb is labeled a tomb that "belonged to a Jesus, doesn't make it the tomb of Jesus Christ," Kloner told *ABC News*.[4]

According to a *Times* (London) report, "The Bishop of Durham has rejected claims in a new television documentary that the tomb of Jesus, Mary and Joseph is in Jerusalem. The Right Rev Dr Tom Wright said: 'What we have to realise is that it is like looking through a London phone book, and seeing the names John and Mary Smith. There are lots of them, just as in Jewish history these other names were very common.'"[5]

Jerusalem-based biblical anthropologist Joe Zias goes a step farther to discredit Cameron's documentary. "What they've done here," Zias says, "is they've simply tried in a very, very dishonest way to try and con the public into believing that this is the tomb of Jesus or Jesus' family. It has nothing whatsoever to do with Jesus."

Zias pointed out a number of contradictions that he says undermines the claim. Jesus was a very common name at the time—Mary even more so. Zias claims 48 percent of women living at the time were named Mary, Mariam or the Hebrew name, Shlomzion.[6] In addition, Jesus' family was poor. Those who paid for the tomb were middle class, at least. If Jesus' family did have the cash, the family tomb would likely have been situated in Nazareth. After all, Jesus was known as Jesus of Nazareth.[7]

The Washington Post shared the concern of viewers regarding this special as well. According to their report, "Scorn for the Discovery Channel's claim to have found the burial place of Jesus, Mary Magdalene and—most explosively—their possible son came not just from Christian scholars but also from Jewish and secular experts who said their judgments were unaffected by any desire to uphold Christian orthodoxy.

"'I'm not a Christian. I'm not a believer. I don't have a dog in this fight,' said William G. Dever, who has been excavating ancient sites in Israel for 50 years and is widely considered the dean of biblical archaeology among U.S. scholars. 'I just think it's a shame the way this story is being hyped and manipulated.'"[8] Dever also said that some of the inscriptions on the Talpiot ossuaries are unclear, but that all of the names are common.

"I've know about these ossuaries for many years and so have many other archaeologists, and none of us thought it was much of a story, because these are rather common Jewish names from that period. It's a publicity stunt, and it will make these guys very rich, and it will upset millions of innocent people because they don't know enough to separate fact from fiction." Similar assessments came from Israeli scholar Amos Kloner, who originally excavated the tomb. Kloner told the *Jerusalem Post* that the documentary is "nonsense." Zias described it in an e-mail to *The Washington Post* as a "hyped up film which is intellectually and scientifically dishonest."[9]

But what did the original American broadcasting audience of *The Lost Tomb of Jesus* of more than 4.1 million viewers really see during the Discovery special?[10] The basic facts include that a tomb was found in Talpiot, Jerusalem with ten bone boxes, called ossuaries. Six of the ten ossuaries have inscriptions. The other four ossuaries have no inscriptions. "The Lost Tomb of Jesus" posits that three of the ossuaries with inscriptions bear the names of figures from the New Testament. The actual meanings of the epigraphs are disputed. The makers of the documentary claim that four leading epigraphers have corroborated their interpretation of the inscriptions.[11] As translated in "The Lost Tomb of Jesus" and *The Jesus Family Tomb*, they read as follows:

- Yeshua bar Yehosef, Aramaic for "Jesus son of Joseph."
- Maria, written in Aramaic script, but a Latin form of the Hebrew name "Miriam" ("Mary")
- Jose, a diminutive of "Joseph" mentioned (in its Greek form "Joses") as the name of one of Jesus' brothers in the New Testament (Mark 6:3).
- Yehuda bar Yeshua, Aramaic for "Judah son of Jesus"
- Mariamene e Mara. According to the filmmakers this is Greek for "Mary known as the master." The similar name "Mariamne" is found in the *Acts of Philip*. Francois Bovon, professor of the history of religion at Harvard University has suggested based on his study of that work that Mariamene, or Mariamne, was the actual name of Mary Magdalene.[12]
- Matia, Hebrew for "Matthew," suggested as a possible husband of one of the women in an unmarked ossuary.[13] The filmmakers claim that there is evidence that Mary mother of Jesus had many relatives named Matthew.

One question many have asked is, "How could so many Americans accept such theories as fact? While there are many aspects to consider, a major reason for this thinking is certainly due to the level of biblical illiteracy in the nation. The article "Americans and the Bible: Bible Ownership, Reading, Study and Knowledge in the United States," written by Michael J. Vlach, reveals startling facts about America's biblical ignorance:

- Only half of adults interviewed nationwide could name any of the four Gospels of the New Testament.
- Just 37% could name all four Gospels.
- Only 42% were able to correctly name five of the Ten Commandments.

- Seven in ten (70%) were able to name the town where Jesus was born, but only 42% could identify Him as the One who delivered the Sermon on the Mount.
- 38% of Americans believe the entire Bible (including the Old Testament) was written several decades after Jesus' death and resurrection.
- 12% of adults believe Noah's wife was Joan of Arc.
- 75% believe the Bible is the origin of the saying "God helps those who help themselves" (actually a saying of Benjamin Franklin).[14]

Current American beliefs about Jesus also provide insight into how people have become more open to such thinking. For instance, in a 2006 survey by religious researcher George Barna, "More than two out of every five adults (41%) believe that when Jesus Christ lived on earth He committed sins."[15] A similar 2005 study revealed that 28% of born again Christians agree that "while he lived on earth, Jesus committed sins, like other people."[16]

The same is true in some of our Christian higher education institutions. Burge points to research at Wheaton College in which the biblical and theological literacy of incoming freshmen have been monitored. These students, who represent almost every Protestant denomination in the United States from every state in the country, have returned some "surprising results":

- One-third could not put the following in order: Abraham, the Old Testament prophets, the death of Christ, and Pentecost.
- Half could not sequence the following: Moses in Egypt, Isaac's birth, Saul's death, and Judah's exile.
- One-third could not identify Matthew as an apostle from a list of New Testament names.
- When asked to locate the biblical book supplying a given story, one-third could not find Paul's travels in Acts, half did not know that the Christmas story was in Matthew, half did not know that the Passover story was in Exodus.[17]

Due to this combination of high-quality documentary arguing against basic biblical beliefs with public ignorance of the Bible's teachings, *The Jesus Family Tomb Controversy* has been written as a guide for navigating the issues of importance in the battle. While this book is in no way an attack against the individuals involved, it is a serious inquiry into the evidence presented to suggest that the Talpiot Tomb actually contains evidence that supports that Jesus of Nazareth and other family members were buried there. My hope is that the information presented in this format will assist those genuinely seeking the truth regarding this disturbing production that claims to be the "greatest archaeological discovery of all time."[8] While it may be, as the back cover of the book claims, "the most controversial archaeological discovery of all time," it is ultimately not because of what was discovered, but by what is being disseminated through the media. *The Jesus Family Tomb*, as we will see, is a major archaeological site, but not for the reasons mentioned by the authors and producers of this event.

Of course, on an issue as heated as the tomb of Jesus, personal bias plays a big role. I've decided to be very up front on this issue.

Dillon's Story

I'm thirty-one years old, married, have two kids, and am involved in my church. I like to play guitar, drink coffee with friends at Starbucks, and write. I grew up in a two-parent, two-income family. My dad worked in construction as a concrete finisher. My mom labored through a conglomeration of jobs over the years as needed to pay the bills. I attended public schools, rode the bus, participated in football and basketball, and even played saxophone in band.

Like many teenagers, I didn't care too much about Jesus until my life was a wreck. Even though my family attended a small church in the area, it wasn't until just before my senior year of high school that I made a committed decision to follow Jesus Christ. I had repeated the prayers and raised my hand at the right time at church, but going through the *motions* was not changing my *emotions*. My way of life definitely wasn't working. I thought I might as well try his.

I returned to my senior year of high school and told my principal I wanted to start a Bible study each morning before school. He nearly fell out of his chair! It was the first time I had ever been to his office without breaking some major rule. By the end of the year, however, several of my friends and I had an early gathering everyday at 7:30 a.m. In May of that year, my same principal even attended a prayer event we sponsored on the morning of the National Day of Prayer.

College was a challenge, to say the least. I changed majors about as often as I did laundry for the first couple of years, finally choosing a "marketable" major called Communications. I figured since "excellent communication skills" were listed in every job ad, majoring in it couldn't hurt.

But something happened again before my senior year of college. Through a bizarre sequence of events, I ended up as an intern with Campus Crusade for Christ, helping gather students to live out their Christian faith on campus. We just called it "Cru." Nothing fancy, just students trying to figure out life and God. The movement quickly grew to well over 50 students during that year, making it one of the largest Christian groups on our campus at the time. My communication skills were now serving a higher purpose.

Based on my friend Gabe's advice and much prayer, my wife Deborah and I finished up our schooling and headed from small town Indiana to downtown Dallas, Texas. We lived in an undersized apartment four blocks from Baylor Hospital. It was great when we had our first kid, but dreadfully noisy when an ambulance took off at three in the morning. Despite the broken sleep patterns, I became a "master of theology" in three quick years while working for various Christian groups.

Following my newly-acquired degree, I headed north of downtown to serve at a medium-sized Bible church and lead teenagers and college students. Unlike any other time in my life, my beliefs were challenged as I dealt with everything from teen suicide to juvenile offenders to straight-A students sharing struggles of doubts about their faith. A teenager catching her dad viewing porn was never discussed in church history. A mom calling at 11 p.m. because she can't find her daughter had not been addressed in any of my textbooks. I learned how to serve the way Jesus did—by helping those in need. Through the ups and downs, those friends became family, providing relationships I cherish still to this day.

Fast-forward to today. I have a gorgeous wife, Deborah, and two awesome kids, Ben and Natalie. A major portion of each day is invested in writing or editing projects for some of today's bestselling Christian authors. My personal struggles still continue at times. Like every other breathing person, I question how God can be at work in the death of a family member. Doubts linger when my bank account runs low. Along the way, I've discovered that in following Jesus the Christian life is certainly not boring. It's an adventure for those who choose it.

My prayer is that you'll consider reading this book with a mind that is curious rather than convinced. I also hope it will be a conversation. I often find myself writing in café's on my laptop. Why? For one, it's the cheapest office space in town. But another advantage is that as I write, I'll often imagine I'm sitting across the coffee table from someone like you to talk about the important issues of life. As you read these words, I hope you'll consider how they connect with your personal life as well as your thinking.

Along the way, feel free to shoot me an email with any insights or questions you have. I will personally respond to you as soon as possible. Just send it to dillon@dillonburroughs.org and check out the latest updates on my Family Tomb of Jesus blog at http://jesusfamilytomb.blogspot.com.

It's All in the Names: Are These Names Really So Special?

The Jesus Family Tomb's foreword begins with the dramatic opening: "What if Jesus didn't exist at all? Today many experts are saying just that."[19] Now, stunning facts have been discovered, according to James Cameron, that deliver "not just a particle of evidence but a veritable avalanche of it."[20] Cameron then shares his personal conclusion by stating:

> Their investigation proves, I believe, beyond any reasonable doubt that a first-century Jewish tomb found in Talpiot, Jerusalem, in 1980 is the tomb of Jesus and his family. What's even more electrifying is what the physical evidence from within the tomb says about Jesus, his death, and his relationships with the other family members found in the same burial site.[21]

Defending Christianity, C.S. Lewis once argued whether Jesus was legend, liar, lunatic, or Lord. Today's arguments take a different approach. "Sure, Jesus lived, but he was human. He may have been a great teacher and even performed some supernatural miracles, but in the end he died. Maybe he even reappeared in a spiritual resurrection, but his body never really came back to life. Therefore, you can call him Lord if you like, but finding his body would not surprise me."

According to the foreword of *The Jesus Family Tomb*, the argument is now not whether Jesus existed, since they claim to have his ossuary. The argument is that he existed, but died like everyone else (or at least only spiritually resurrected). Not only that, they suggest to have proof based on the names of other family members, including the suggestion that they also have Mary the mother of Jesus, Mary Magdalene as the wife of Jesus, and their child named Jude. The suggestion flies in contrast with everything known in the four Gospels and early church history, yet it is claimed as "fact" because of a handful of name inscriptions. In other words, "it's all in the names."

If the names in the Talpiot Tomb could be shown to belong to people other than claimed in *The Jesus Family Tomb*, then the conclusion fails to work. To state it logically:

1. If the Jesus, son of Joseph inscription does not belong to Jesus,
2. Then the ossuary did not belong to Jesus.

This is a big "if" that must be considered seriously. Yet, the "ifs" get bigger. To make the theory of this special work, the following must also be true:

1. If Maria is the mother of Jesus, Mariamne is Mary Magdalene, if Jude is the child of Jesus, if Matthew is related to the family, if Jose is the brother of Jesus, if all of the ossuaries included related family members, if the disciples and hundreds of eyewitnesses were lying about the resurrection, if Jesus' family was buried in Jerusalem instead of their hometown of Nazareth, and if the predictions from the Old Testament and Jesus were wrong about his resurrection,
2. THEN the Jesus ossuary might really belong to Jesus of Nazareth.

One of the most insightful comments in the panel discussion led by Ted Koppel following the television special was when Darrell Bock noted how the "theories" were strung together as if all true to prove the conclusion. He stated, ""I just don't think you can connect these dots."

In this chapter, we'll take a brief look at each of the names discovered in the Talpiot Tomb. Many of these names will be discussed further in later chapters, but for now, our purpose will be to look at the basic information regarding each name and its significance in driving the theory behind *The Lost Tomb of Jesus*.

Jesus son of Joseph

The most important of the names discovered is clearly the ossuary claimed as Yeshua bar Yehosef, Aramaic for "Jesus son of Joseph." Is this really the bone box of the same Jesus discussed in the Gospels?

First, let's begin with the handwriting itself. The documentary suggests that "it is clear" that the reading is correct at Jesus, son of Joseph. Several scholars disagree on this "certainty," yet their viewpoints are not even noted on the program.

The *Jerusalem Post* notes that,

> "One of those Jacobovici didn't consult was Joseph Naveh, the preeminent Israeli epigrapher. Yet when I went to see Naveh at his Jerusalem home on Tuesday, the emeritus professor peered intently at the markings scratched into the side of the ossuary in the color photograph I'd brought him and pronounced, almost instantaneously: 'Jesus son of Joseph.'
>
> "He did then qualify himself, but only a little: 'The "Joseph" is unmistakable,' he said. 'The "son of" is okay. And you can certainly read it as "Jesus," he said. 'Just not definitely. There are lots of additional lines here that don't belong.'
>
> "Another prominent expert whom Jacobovici did not consult, across town in the tranquil offices of the French Biblical and Archeological School in east Jerusalem, was Prof. Emile Puech. His response to the inscription was much the same as Naveh's. 'It's very crude lettering,' said the bearded, French-born Father Puech.
>
> "And a third leading authority, Ada Yardeni, also essentially came down on Jacobovici's side. "'Son of Joseph,' for sure," she said after an inspection. 'The first name? Well, there are lots of markings here, but, yes, it could well be Jesus.'" [22]

American scholars are also divided on the issue. For instance, Dr. Craig Evans, New Testament scholar and researcher on *The Gospel of Judas*, comments that:

> There are several problems with this radical and new interpretation of the Talpiot Tomb. *First*, the name *Jesus* in the "Jesus(?), son of Joseph" inscription is far from certain. Some experts think it is actually a different name. Kloner, followed by Rahmani, reads "Yeshua'(?)." They are unsure of the reading. If the first name is not Yeshua' (or Jesus), then the new theory collapses. The facsimile of this inscription indicates why epigraphers find the first name (or word) uncertain. I can make out the last two words, "son of Jehosef [or Joseph]" but I can't see Yeshua [Images of this inscription are available at this article's website.].[23]

Dr. Stephen Pfann of the University of the Holy Land in Israel is also unsure that the name "Jesus" on the caskets was read correctly. He thinks it's more likely the name "Hanun." In his professional opinion, ancient Semitic script is notoriously difficult to decipher.[24]

Concerning the inscription attributed to Jesus son of Joseph, Steve Caruso, a professional Aramaic translator using a computer to visualize different interpretations, claims that although it is *possible* to read it as "Yeshua" that "overall it is a very strong possibility that this inscription is not."[25]

In this very first name, the entire theory stands or falls. If this name is not Jesus, then case closed. Perhaps this is why the documentary suggests their conclusion is so certain. This is the first "if" required to make the theory stand, and even it stands on shaky ground.

Maria

Maria, written in Aramaic script, but a Latin form of the Hebrew name "Miriam," is suggested as the same Mary as the mother of Jesus. While the name is not disputed in this case, the connection is. According to statistics on first-century ossuaries, as many as 21 percent of female ossuary names included a form of the name Mary. This means that one out of every five first century tombs included the name Mary. Why should it be assumed that such a common name is Mary mother of Jesus? What proof exists? The documentary claims this is the same Mary based on the *other* ossuaries, not solely on the Maria inscription. Therefore, it's strength stands or falls based on analysis of the other names in the tomb.

Jose

Jose is a diminutive of "Joseph." Because its Greek form is Joses, the documentary connects it with Joses, the brother of Jesus listed in Mark 6:3. Again, the name identification is dependent upon the connection of the so-called "Jesus son of Joseph" inscription as being the same as Jesus of Nazareth. According to Craig Evans, the reading Joseh, said to agree with the name of Jesus' brother given in Mark 6:3; 15:40, 47 is also problematic. The spelling YSH should be vocalized Josah. If so, this connection fails, altering the likelihood that this is the tomb of Jesus' family greatly.

In addition, as a resident of Nazareth, one has to believe Joses was buried in a location far outside of his hometown for this theory to work, despite the fact that we lack evidence that he ever lived in Jerusalem.

Judah son of Jesus

The one child-sized ossuary is one that includes the inscription, Yehuda bar Yeshua, Aramaic for "Judah son of Jesus." The major problem with this inscription is the argument from silence. Judah and Jesus (Yeshua) were both very common names. It would be the modern equivalent of "John, son of Robert." Without additional information, such as a town name, other family members, markings on the tomb, or other identifying features, there is nothing to base a conclusion upon.

Furthermore, the suggestion that Jesus had a son stands in contrast with all of the existing documentation from the first two hundred years of Christianity. It is interesting to note that according to more recent research, it has been observed that nearly *all* Jewish and non-Jewish literature discovered up to 200 A.D. from the area where Jesus lived mentions Jesus or Christianity. This is exactly the *opposite* of what many have traditionally questioned—"If Jesus was so important, why didn't more ancient writers mention him?" The answer is that they did.

For instance, the Jewish Talmud and Jewish historian Josephus both mention Jesus, though both were Jewish writings. If they had known of a wife or child of Jesus, it is likely they would have been mentioned. Of the Greco-Roman sources, there are seven writings that mention Christianity, sometimes in a very derogatory fashion. Yet even in the most negative criticisms, nothing is mentioned of a family. While these arguments are based on a lack of documentation, the fact that all of the early information mentions Jesus as single and without children is a strong indication that the New Testament record on this matter is true.

No mention at all is made of the fact that though we only have a few hundred ossuaries with inscribed names, yet there is in fact another ossuary with the inscription 'Jesus son of Joseph.' Apparently this was not a rare combination of names at all, and in any case, as I have said Jesus of Nazareth is never called 'son of Joseph' by his family, or by his disciples. Notice how Luke pours cold water on that theory in Luke 3:21: "Now Jesus himself was about 30 when he began his ministry, he was the son, so it was supposed/thought, of Joseph." Supposed by whom? Clearly not by Luke or the family whom Luke has just shown knew about the virginal conception of Jesus. Even the cousins knew about this miracle when Mary told Elizabeth. There can be no good reason Luke would put it this way if he knew the earliest followers of Jesus or members of his family had thought that Jesus was son of Joseph.[26]

Mariamene e Mara

Mariamene e Mara is the name the filmmakers claim belongs to Mary Magdalene. Where do they find evidence for this claim? The only source text is *The Gospel of Philip*, a book from the fourth century. Relying on this book, which was written at least two hundred fifty years after the lifetimes of the events by an unknown writer other than the apostle Philip, the documentary claims Mariamene was her real name.

Here's how critical New Testament scholar Cross replied in an e-mail to the *National Review*: "I am skeptical about Jacobovici's claims, not because of a faulty reading of the ossuary which reads yeshua' bar yosep [Jesus son of Joseph] I believe, but because the onomasticon [list of proper names] in his period in Jerusalem is exceedingly narrow. Patriarchal names and biblical names repeat ad *nauseam*. It has been reckoned that 25% of feminine names in this period were Maria/Miryam, etc., that is variants of Mary. So the cited statistics are unpersuasive. You know the saying: lies, damned lies, and statistics."[27]

Again, the historical facts are lacking. According to the website Extreme Theology:

> In order to make the claim that Mariamne is Mary Magdalene the film's producers have literally had to manufacture evidence and ignore practically every established rule that relates to historical evidence and primary source documents.
>
> The ONLY way the film's producers could build their case is by setting aside the eye-witness testimony of the New Testament Gospels which never once refer to Mary Magdalene as Mariamne. They instead favor an obscure 4th century Gnostic document called the Acts of Philip in order to make their claim that Mary Magdalene and the Mariamne of the Talpiot Tomb are one in the same.
>
> By doing this, the film's producers are literally expecting us to believe that a document written nearly 300 years after Jesus and Mary Magdalene walked the Earth is MORE credible and MORE accurate than the New Testament

documents which were written by eye-witnesses VERY shortly after the events they record. This is absurd!

Furthermore, if you actually take the time to read the Acts of Philip you will notice some very funny things. The first thing you'll notice is that the book itself very fanciful. The book's narrative claims that Jesus sent out a group of followers to spread his message. The followers were Philip, Bartholomew, and a woman named Mariamne who is identified as Philip's sister. Among their accomplishments was the conversion of a talking leopard, a talking goat, and the slaying of a dragon. Yes, that is right Bartholomew, Philip and Mariamne went out preaching Jesus' message <u>to talking leopard's and talking goats</u>!

Secondly, the Acts of Philip <u>NEVER even ONCE</u> refers to Mariamne as Mary Magdalene. Granted, some scholars speculate that Mariamne COULD be Mary Magdalene BUT the text never actually says that. Therefore, the film's producers are literally overstating the evidence supplied to us in the Acts of Philip.[28]

Another interesting dispute revolves around the mention of a writing by Hippolytus. At one juncture we are told that the name Mariamenon is found in Hippolytus, a second century church historian. According to New Testament professor Dr. Ben Witherington of Asbury Seminary in Wilmore, Kentucky, there are:

"Two problems with this. Firstly so far as I can see, that name never occurs in the works of Hippolytus (and the name Mariamene is not the same name, see the previous post with Richard Bauckham's analysis of the names). Secondly, Hippolytus died in about A.D. 236. He comes to us from the end of the second century A.D. He could never have known any eywitnesses or even second-third generation followers of Jesus. Even if he did mention the name in question (the one on the ossuary found at Talpiot), he provides no early second century evidence for this name, much less for the theory that this name is one way of referring to Mary Magdalene. In fact the Acts of Philip, at best a fourth century document is the basis of the theory of Prof. Bovon that Mariamenon= Mary Magdalene, but nowhere in that document are the two equated. The woman referred to in that document is an evangelist in Greek who is the sister of Philip (whether Philip the apostle or the later Philip the evangelist found in Acts 8, we could debate). In other words, we have no hard evidence at all that equates Mary Magdalene with this particular name, or even with the later figure found in the Acts of Philip. There is then certainly no first or second century evidence that Mary Magdalene was every called by the name on the Talpiot ossuary, or would have been labeled this on a first century A.D. ossuary. And why again would her inscription be in Greek, and all the other ones in the tomb in Aramaic or Hebrew? We are not told.[29]

To claim the name fits Mary Magdalene twists the name's meaning in ways no previous generation of scholars has attempted. We'll see more on this in the chapter on Mary Magdalene.

Matia (or Matya)

Lastly, the tomb contains an ossuary with the name Matia (or Matya), Hebrew for "Matthew." Yet there is no Matthew listed as a brother of Jesus or contemporary family member of the family. In addition, it would not make sense for this Matthew to be the apostle Matthew who penned the first gospel. Yet the filmmakers claim that there is evidence that Mary mother of Jesus had many relatives named Matthew, citing Luke 3 for proof.

The narrator of the television special notes that "There is reason to believe there were many Matthews in Jesus' family." Dr. Tabor claims there were as many as eight Matthews in Luke 3. However, a look at the verses in question could only sustain six Matthews at the most if every near variant is included. Yet none of those mentioned would fit the time frame of the Matia in the Talpiot Tomb. Once again, based on very little evidence, the "decision" was made that Matthew was a member of Jesus' family.

One additional interesting fact was that in the statistical analysis, the Matthew ossuary was left out of the numbers. Why? The documentary and book both state that since they were not sure how to rate it, it was left out in order not to "skew" the numbers. Yet if all of those in the tomb were related, as they claim, then Matthew must be taken into account. To leave him out causes the statistics to favor those creating the statistics and once again reveals the bias of those developing the numbers.

One article on this topic well noted the overall observations regarding the names by stating that the names on the ossuaries were very common at that time based upon:

> "Charlesworth of Princeton Theological Seminary says he has a first-century letter written by someone named Jesus, addressed to someone else named Jesus and witnessed by a third party named Jesus." This demonstrates the commonality of the name Jesus. Isn't it likely that other names would be common as well? Think about it. The name "Mary" occurs in the gospels several times in reference to different women. Also, if Christianity was on the rise in the culture, it makes sense that people would adopt Christian names as they eagerly moved away from the imposing Roman Empire's rule. This would increase the name frequency.
>
> "'Jesus' and 'Joseph' were common names of the time, and another ossuary bearing the same inscription [Jesus son of Joseph] was revealed by archaeologist Eleazar Levi Sukenik in a 1931 lecture in Berlin. However, this ossuary is set apart by its presence in a tomb alongside others bearing names associated with Jesus' family..." The fact is that "Jesus son of Joseph" exists elsewhere in archaeological findings.
>
> Nearly 25% of the Jewish women in the first-century Judea had the same name of Mary according to some studies. Again, this is evidence of a very common name usage.[30] Jesus and Mary (or variations of the name Mary) were among the most common names in 1st-century Israel. "That's like saying John and Mary in our country," said Charles Dyer, a Bible scholar and dean of Moody Bible Institute in Chicago. "There is not a shred of evidence that that tomb and those ossuaries were connected with the Jesus and Mary that we know."[31]

When Israeli archaeologist Amos Kloner first discovered the Talpiot Tomb in 1980, he found the tomb and the ossuaries interesting but of no particular archaeological importance. He said there are more than 900 buried tombs just like the Jesus tomb within a two-mile radius of Talpiot. Of them, 71 bear the name Jesus and two include the phrase "Jesus, son of Joseph." The tomb in Talpiot is one of them. But the inscription, he said, was barely decipherable and therefore questionable.[32]

Others agree with Kloner's perspective. "Prominent scholars call that shoddy science, and Zias says as many as 200 people were likely buried in the same tomb, making the six uncovered names a meaningless sample. 'I think they're mainly attempting to exploit *The Da Vinci Code*,' says Harvard archeologist Lawrence Stager, noting there were 71 Jesuses buried in the cemetery where the boxes were found. 'I would describe this as a sheep-and-donkey show.'"[33]

In the end, *The Jesus Family Tomb* is all about the names. If this suggested cast of characters is true, Christianity is in trouble. But even a cursory analysis reveals that the trouble falls on the side trying to prove the Talpiot Tomb as the tomb of Jesus and his family. In our next chapter, we'll discuss this issue of names even further, noting that there are three languages involved in this tomb, complicating matters even further.

Nimble Books LLC

Multilingual Madness: Why Are There Three Languages in One Tomb?

Beyond the simple fact that the names in the tomb are difficult to read and interpret, there is the issue that there are three distinct languages used on only six ossuary boxes in the Talpiot Tomb. The big question is, why? Further, does the use of three languages help or hurt the case of the *Lost Tomb of Jesus* producers who claim their particular identification of names?

What Languages Are Included?

A quick run-down of the names on the Talpiot Tomb ossuaries reveals that three of the ossuaries are written in Aramaic, two in Hebrew, and one in Greek:

- Aramaic: Jesus, James, and Judah
- Hebrew: Maria and Matthew
- Greek: Mariamne e Mara

What options exist for the inclusion of these three languages? First, one possibility is that different individuals from different background were buried in this tomb. For instance, with its markings and clearly affluent level of care, perhaps it was some sort of royal tomb, including community leaders from different families.

Another possibility lies behind the historical tradition that families used the same tomb and ossuaries for generations. If true in the case of the Talpiot Tomb, then perhaps different generations included names with different languages. This would especially apply to the Aramaic and Hebrew names, as they were closely related languages.

In either case, one would expect the DNA of the individuals to show they were not directly related, especially in the case of mitochondrial DNA.[34] According to Dr. Ben Witherington:

> There is a major problem with the analysis of the names on these ossuaries. By this I mean one has to explain why one is in Hebrew, several are in Aramaic, but the supposed Mary Magdalene ossuary is in Greek. This suggests a multi-generation tomb, not a single generation tomb, and indeed a tomb that comes from after A.D. 70 after the Romans had destroyed the temple mount and Jewish Christians fled the city. This tomb is not in old Jerusalem. It is nowhere near the Temple mount, and we already know that the tomb of James was near the Temple Mount. The earliest Jewish Christians in Jerusalem, including the members of Jesus' family and Mary Magdalene, did not speak Greek. They spoke Aramaic. We have absolutely no historical evidence to suggest Mary Magdalene would have been called by a Greek name before A.D. 70. She grew up in a Jewish fishing village called Migdal, not a Greek city at all. It makes no sense that her ossuary would have a Greek inscription and that of her alleged husband an Aramaic inscription.[35]

The multiple languages involved would also become problematic in the documentary's handling of the ossuary they claim belongs to Mary Magdalene. As one article observes:

> The film claims that "Maraimne e Mara" means Mary the Master. But the only way they could make this claim is if they mix languages. Mara means master in Aramaic, but the ossuary inscription is written in Greek. In order for the film makers to be correct about the ossuary text reading "Mary the Master" we have to believe that the inscription although written in Greek is supposed to be understood as being half Greek and half Aramaic. This is preposterous. Since the inscription is in Greek, if it was supposed to say "Mary the Master" it would have to say "Mariamne Ho Kurios" NOT "Mariamne e Mara."[36]

How can the same documentary argue that the Greek name means Mary Magdalene yet the "Mara" portion means "master" in Aramaic and therefore means Mary the Master? It can't be both. If it's Mary the Master, then it's not Greek. But it's clearly in Greek, so it cannot mean "master."

Furthermore, Dr. Craig Evans of Arcadia Divinity School writes:

> *Secondly*, almost no one agrees that the name *Mariamne* refers to Mary Magdalene, or that *Mara* means "Lady" or "Master," as though it were a title of honor. It is, rather, an abbreviation of Martha, which is attested in other inscriptions. Given that the Greek form of Mariamne is in the genitive case, the inscription could be interpreted "Mariamne's (daughter) Mara (or Martha)." Kloner and Rahmani translate: "[Ossuary] of Mariamne, (who is also called) Mara."[37]

In this analysis, we find two more likely options for the name Mary Magdalene based on its actual linguistic usage. Both options refer to names that could not refer to Mary Magdalene. Yet where were these scholarly opinions in the television special or book? They were completely left out. Again, the most solid options based on the language show this tomb could not hold Mary Magdalene, meaning the entire theory of Jesus' family falls apart.

Additional Scenarios

There are several more likely reconstructions in this tomb scene that are not mentioned elsewhere. I have listed these in no particular order. They are simply to show what other options exist and how many options exist for this tomb.

OPTION 1: EACH LANGUAGE REFERS TO A DIFFERENT FAMILY

In this case, the Aramaic names—Jesus, James, and Judah—would refer to names in one family. Jesus, father of Judah, with James as a brother or related to other unnamed ossuaries in the tomb. With four additional unnamed ossuaries, two could be wives of the two adult men. This is only a theory, but is possible.

The two Hebrew names—Maria and Matthew—may have been a couple as well. This would leave as many as four other ossuaries that could have been related. Either children, siblings, or parents could have been in the unnamed ossuaries.

The Greek name, Mariamne e Mara, could have had a husband in one of the unnamed ossuaries or may have married into one of the other families. Complicating the matter further, Israeli archaeologist Amos Kloner, the person who originally researched the tomb in 1980, stated in an interview recently that it is also possible for family servants who were close to the family to be buried with family members. Therefore, even beyond direct family members, servants may be included in this tomb.[38]

OPTION 2: THE MULTIPLE LANGUAGES INVOLVE A MULTILINGUAL FAMILY

This option somewhat fits the view presented in the documentary, but holds room for much variation. If this is one family for instance, is it from one generation, or two or more generations? Without dating the ossuaries and their remains, there is no way to know for certain. Second, even if it is one family, this family may have consisted of blood family members, in-laws, extended family, and even servants.

However, against this option is that it is also possible that the inscriptions being in three different languages do not necessarily suggest the idea that the remains are from three different generations. It is true that the author of the *Gospel of Thomas* author used the pseudonym Didymus Judas Thomas, three names in the same three different languages.

OPTION 3: THE TOMB WAS DESIGNED FOR THOSE WITH THE ABILITY TO AFFORD IT

It has been noted by some articles on the Lost Tomb of Jesus that the only people who had ossuaries and a tomb as nice as the one in Talpiot would be those with a fairly high level of affluence. If space was an issue (which could have been the case with as many as 900 tombs within a two-mile radius in Talpiot), then it may have functioned like modern cemeteries, where space is given to those with the money to afford it.

OPTION 4: THE TOMB INSCRIPTIONS WERE FORGED

I personally don't believe this to be the case, but there are those who have claimed forgery for the James ossuary because it claims to belong to the brother of Jesus. It is only reasonable to assume some will suggest the same regarding the Talpiot Tomb. However, there is no need to push for this view. Even if all of the inscriptions are authentic (which seems to be the case), there is still plenty of room for debate regarding their readings and interpretation.

OPTION 5: THE DIFFERENT LANGUAGES ARE DUE TO DIFFERENT GENERATIONS

As mentioned in passing in option one above, since tombs were used for several generations, it is possible that the different languages resulted from changes in the family over multiple generations within the family. Think about it: the documentary did not mention an age comparison of the different ossuaries other than a first century date due to the style of tomb. If dating could be measured of the different ossuaries, what would happen to the theory if the dates were 50 or 100 years apart? It could make a tremendous difference in the conclusions drawn. Again, this is not proven, but it is a possibility.

On another historical note, we find that:

> We should note that the surviving six names are only six of many more who were buried in this family tomb. There may have been as many as 35. The six people whose names we have could have belonged to as many as four different generations. This is a large family tomb, which would certainly have been used for quite some time by the same family. We should not imagine a small family group. Some members of the family of Jesus we know lived in Jerusalem for only three decades (from the death of Jesus to the execution of his brother James in 62). None of our other evidence would suggest that there were so many of them as to require a tomb of this size.[39]

Bock agrees that the age of the boxes fits the time period of Christ. "Ossuaries were used for only about a century, from about 14 B.C. to 70 A.D.," he says. "You buried a body, it decomposed and you put the bones in the ossuary after a year or so." But he points out that the Jesus box is crudely done with graffiti-like inscriptions. Wouldn't Jesus' followers have prepared something more reverential?[40]

Frank Moore Cross, a professor emeritus in the Department of Near Eastern Languages and Civilizations at Harvard University, told *Discovery News*, "The inscriptions are from the Herodian Period (which occurred from around 1 B.C. to 1 A.D.). The use of limestone ossuaries and the varied script styles are characteristic of that time."[41]

Witherington agrees, but suggests a broad dating to include the scope of the possible dates of the tomb:

> It is therefore my tentative suggestion that the Talpiot tomb may well be an early Jewish tomb not connected with the followers of Jesus, but it could also be an early Christian tomb from a generation subsequent to the time of Jesus. And what we know about those Christians is that they related to each other as family, even when they were not physically related, and were in some cases buried together, not in clan tombs, because their religious families were more important to them than their physical ones. This tomb may reflect that later Christian practice and reality. It would be nice if the other ossuaries from the Talpiot tomb could be DNA tested so we could find out if any of the folks in this tomb were related. We do not know. But it would not surprise me if none of them were. The practice of osslegium, or burial in ossuaries, continued on after A.D. 70 until the Bar Kokhba revolt at least. There is no reason why this Talpiot tomb might not reflect the period between A.D. 70 and 125 or so.[42]

In conclusion, the multiple languages could be due to any one of a multitude of scenarios. For a documentary to present only one scenario while neglecting a multitude of additional perspectives and pieces of evidence presents a one-sided viewpoint that comes across as factual although it is in fact misleading.

Hometown Heroes: Wasn't Jesus from Nazareth?

It's the "of Nazareth" part that is one of the many significant flaws in the documentary's thesis, said Darrell Bock, a professor of New Testament studies at Dallas Theological Seminary. "The simple way to say this is that there is no reason why a family tomb of Jesus' family, who was from Galilee, would be in Jerusalem," said Bock, who has seen a pre-release version of the documentary. Nazareth, in Galilee, is about 85 miles from Jerusalem. "That's a four-day walk," Bock said.

"For their scenario to be true, you've got to believe that pilgrims went down to Jerusalem for Passover, where their leader, Jesus, was crucified—by surprise—and his followers secretly buy this tomb space . . . steal the body, bury the body, and then a year later, for someone that they revered, put his bones in an ossuary with the name written in graffiti-type script," he said. "And then they go out and preach that the tomb was empty and everything they present as true is false."[43]

According to the New Testament, Nazareth was the home of Joseph and Mary and the site of the Annunciation (Luke 1:26), when Mary was told by the Angel Gabriel that she would have Jesus as her son. Nazareth is also traditionally accepted to be where Jesus grew up from his childhood to manhood (Luke 2:39).

In John 1:46, Nathaniel asks, "Can anything good come out of Nazareth?" The meaning of this cryptic question is debated. Some commentators suggest that it means Nazareth was very small and unimportant. But others suggest that the question does not speak of Nazareth's size but of its *goodness*. In fact, Nazareth was viewed with hostility by the evangelists, for it did not believe in Jesus and "he could do no mighty work there" (Mark 6:5).

In all four gospels we read the famous saying, "A prophet is not without honor except in his own country, and among his own kin, and in his own house" (Matthew 13:57; Mark 6:4; Luke 4:24; John 4:44). In one verse the

Nazarenes even attempt to kill Jesus by throwing him off a cliff (Luke 4:29). Nazareth, being the home of those near and dear to Jesus, apparently suffered negatively in relation to this doctrine. Therefore, Nathanael's question, "Can anything good come out of Nazareth?" is consistent with a negative view of Nazareth in the canonical gospels, and with the fact that even Jesus' brothers did not believe him (John 7:5).[44] At the time of Jesus, Nazareth was a small town, estimated in size anywhere from 480 to 2,000 people.[45]

Nazareth in History

According to one historical source on the origins of Nazareth, the ancient settlement at Nazareth was probably left in ruins about 733 B.C. when Tiglath-Pileser II, the Assyrian conqueror, swept through Galilee. Taking most of the citizens of the Northern Kingdom into exile in Assyria, he replaced them with people from the countries he had conquered. Isaiah's lament had come to pass, "In the past He humbled the land of Zebulon and the land of Naphtali," leaving the region to be called "Galilee of the Gentiles" (Isaiah 9:1). As the Maccabean era opened in 167 B.C., only a few isolated Jewish groups were living in Galilee. The Hasmonean conquest of the region by John Hyrcanus (134-104 B.C.), however, opened the way for a significant immigration of Jews from Babylon and Persia. Further, Hyrcanus and his successors forced Gentiles in the region to convert to Judaism or be expelled. By Jesus' time, the Jewish population predominated in Galilee, as witnessed by the number of synagogues He encountered during His ministry throughout the territory.[46]

Nazareth in the New Testament

It is also interesting to note that the town of Nazareth was only mentioned in the Bible in the four Gospels and the Book of Acts. Used a total of 28 times, its references include:

1. Angel announces the birth of Jesus to Mary in Nazareth (Luke 1:26).
2. Jesus' family moves back to Nazareth from Egypt after Herod's death (Matthew 2:23; Luke 2:39).
3. Jesus and his family returned to Nazareth after the temple visit (Luke 2:51).
4. Jesus came from Nazareth to be baptized by John the Baptist (Mark 1:9).
5. Jesus spoke at the synagogue in his hometown of Nazareth (Luke 4:16).
6. Jesus left Nazareth to begin preaching in other towns in fulfillment of prophecy (Matthew 4:13).
7. At the event traditionally called Palm Sunday, Jesus was called by the people, "This is Jesus, the prophet from Nazareth in Galilee" (Matthew 21:11).
8. Jesus was called Jesus of Nazareth, meaning this was the place people knew he was from (Matthew 26:71).
9. Demons address Jesus as "Jesus of Nazareth" (Mark 1:24; Luke 4:34).
10. Bartimaeus yells to him as Jesus of Nazareth (Mark 10:47).
11. People call him "Jesus of Nazareth" to a blind beggar (Luke 18:37).
12. Jesus is called "Jesus of Nazareth" by the two men on the road to Emmaus (Luke 24:20).
13. Philip calls Jesus "Jesus of Nazareth" (John 1:45).
14. Nazareth considered an insignificant town (John 1:46).
15. Those seeking to arrest Jesus call him "Jesus of Nazareth" (John 18:5, 7).
16. The sign on the cross of Jesus called him "Jesus of Nazareth" John 19:19).
17. Peter calls Jesus "Jesus of Nazareth" when speaking of him in Jerusalem (Acts 2:22; 3:6; 4:10).
18. Those who spoke against Stephen at his court trial called Jesus "Jesus of Nazareth" (Acts 6:14).

19. Peter calls Jesus "Jesus of Nazareth" when speaking with Cornelius and his family (Acts 10:38).
20. Paul called Jesus "Jesus of Nazareth" in his testimony and preaching (Acts 22:9; 26:9).

Geographically, Nazareth is situated among the southern ridges of Lebanon, on the steep slope of a hill, about 14 miles from the Sea of Galilee and about 6 west from Mount Tabor. It is identified with the modern village *en-Nazirah*. It lies "as in a hollow cup" lower down upon the hill than the ancient city. The main road for traffic between Egypt and the interior of Asia passed by Nazareth near the foot of Tabor, and thence northward to Damascus.[47]

Nazareth in the Tomb Special

Joe Zias, the curator of the Rockefeller Museum in Jerusalem from 1971-1997, has provided a full review on the Tomb of Jesus controversy. A few quotes regarding the issue of Nazareth include:[48]

> The film's 'experts' include several of whom hold academic positions with proven track records in every field except Biblical Archaeology. Most experts however have no creditability within the profession. Charles Pellegrino is an example of this. His past books are *The Ghosts of Atlantis, Ghosts of Vesuvius, Return to Sodom and Gomorrah*, and *Unearthing Atlantis*. The first two deal with psychic phenomena while the last two deal with mythical places. He co-authored the book as well as appears from time to time in the film.
>
> The important thing to remember here is that individuals outside of Judea, buried in Judea were named according to their place of origin, whereas in Judea this was not necessary. Had the names been Jesus of Nazareth, Mary of Nazareth, Joseph of Nazareth etc I would have been totally convinced that this may be the family tomb, but as none of the names have place of origin, they are all Judeans.[49]

Jodi Magness, an archaeologist at the University of North Carolina at Chapel Hill, also expressed irritation that the claims were made at a news conference rather than in a peer-reviewed scientific article. By going directly to the media, she said, the filmmakers "have set it up as if it's a legitimate academic debate, when the vast majority of scholars who specialize in archaeology of this period have flatly rejected this," she said.

Magness noted that at the time of Jesus, wealthy families buried their dead in tombs cut by hand from solid rock, putting the bones in niches in the walls and then, later, transferring them to ossuaries. She said Jesus came from a poor family that, like most Jews of the time, probably buried their dead in ordinary graves. "If Jesus' family had been wealthy enough to afford a rock-cut tomb, it would have been in Nazareth, not Jerusalem," she said.

Magness also said the names on the Talpiot ossuaries indicate that the tomb belonged to a family from Judea, the area around Jerusalem, where people were known by their first name and father's name. As Galileans, Jesus and his family members would have used their first name and home town, she said. "This whole case [for the tomb of Jesus] is flawed from beginning to end."[50]

Traditional thinking would be that families were buried in their home towns. In this case it would have been Nazareth, not Jerusalem. Jesus was known as Jesus of Nazareth. If this really is the tomb of the biblical Jesus and his family, then why they be buried somewhere other than his hometown, Nazareth? This would have gone against Jewish culture and custom.

Also, shouldn't the burial inscription have read "Jesus of Nazareth" or "Jesus of Nazareth, son of Joseph" if it were the Jesus of the New Testament? At least to decide with any form of certainty, more evidence would be needed, especially with a tomb a four day journey from the family's hometown.

There was a two day burial window under Jewish law. This meant that a person had to be buried within two days of death. Therefore, he might not be buried in his hometown. However, after the body decomposed and only the bones were left, it would appropriate to move them. Since ossuaries contained only bones, why is it located in Jerusalem and not Nazareth?[51]

In the documentary, this conflict is noted by claiming that the Talpiot Tomb is between Jerusalem and Bethlehem. As a king, he would be buried in or near Jerusalem. As a descendant of the family of David, he would be buried near Jerusalem. However, which is it? The tomb is not in Bethlehem. It is in the Talpiot area of Jerusalem. This still does not answer the question.

"One of the objections from an Israeli curator," Bock says, "is that Jesus' family tomb would not have been in Jerusalem but Galilee. And to be able to use a secret family tomb, they would have had to have the money to do it. [The documentary] tried to go through all the objections, and they did answer some of them. But just because you answer the question doesn't mean the answer is persuasive."[52]

NIMBLE BOOKS LLC

There's DNA! It Must Be True... What Does the DNA Test Prove?

Chapter 13 of *The Family Tomb of Jesus* begins early with a bold assertion that:

> If these two ossuaries truly belong to Jesus and Mary Magdalene, DNA tests would reveal that the two people buried within were *not* related. All scriptural records—whether canonical or apocryphal—were clear on one genealogical point: Jesus of Nazareth and Mary Magdalene, if their DNA could be read, would be two individuals who had no family ties. But what are the alternatives? People buried in the same tomb were related by either blood or marriage.[53]

The authors' first point—that the DNA would show they were unrelated—seems rather obvious. Two married individuals would not have the same genetic makeup of, say, a brother or sister. Humorously, they point out that the scriptures "were clear" that Jesus and Mary Magdalene were not related. However, it's their question that follows that comes under scrutiny. What are the alternatives? The authors claim that everyone in the tomb would be related by blood or marriage. Is this true?

We have already noted earlier in this book that servants were sometimes buried with family members. In addition, just for argument's sake, let's assume that these two individuals were Jesus and Mary Magdalene. Couldn't Mary have been married any of the men in the Talpiot Tomb? Of course! But it's definitely not as spicy as connecting Jesus and Mary Magdalene. Then, that doesn't even take into consideration that the so-called Mary Magdalene ossuary could be a distant relative, such as a niece/nephew type of relationship. The possibilities are numerous, even if the right people were identified (which is another problem altogether). Where were these options in the book and film?

"The DNA testing is interesting," Bock says. "It sounds like the woman in the box is not biologically related to the person named Jesus in the other box. If it's a family tomb they have hit, that makes sense. But that doesn't tell you whose family it is. It proves absolutely nothing. But because we have invoked the magical forensics of DNA it sounds impressive."[54]

In an interview, Simcha Jacobovici was asked why the filmmakers did not conduct DNA testing on the other ossuaries to determine whether the one inscribed "Judah, son of Jesus" was genetically related to either the Jesus or Mary Magdalene boxes; or whether the Jesus remains were actually the offspring of Mary. His response? "We're not scientists. At the end of the day we can't wait till every ossuary is tested for DNA," he said. "We took the story that far. At some point you have to say, 'I've done my job as a journalist.'"[55] Yet Ted Koppel's own correspondence with the DNA lab, and with the statistician reported in the follow up debate finds those folks doing their best to distance themselves from the conclusions of the show, and insisting that it is only a remote possibility.[56]

The argument that Jesus was married or had a child comes solely from silence. No New Testament document speaks of such relationships, nor do Christian or secular writings from the early centuries of Christianity. The closest document is the apocryphal *Gospel of Philip*, written approximately 275 A.D., written neither by the apostle nor in the time period of the New Testament. As my coauthored book *The Da Vinci Code Controversy*[57] notes, even the passage used to suggest a married Jesus is used grossly out of context.

The film and book also make a distinction regarding the type of DNA tested. Again, in the book version, we are told:

> Matheson then explained that after extraction the *nuclear* DNA in the bones—the broader genetic blueprint copied in the nucleus of every cell—had prove extremely difficult to recover. Impossible, in fact, given 2006 technology.
>
> "However," Matheson said, "we did not quit. Instead, we shifted our focus to the mitochondrial DNA—which is, of course, the DNA inherited maternally, from mother to child. This means that we can identify maternal relationships.[58]

Ultimately, the book chronicles the adventure of discovering that these two samples did not share the same type of mitochondrial DNA. What had they really found? In *The Jesus Family Tomb*, after a brief section break, we are thrown a brief curveball. Suddenly, readers are challenged to consider Mary Magdalene, "the companion of Jesus," in a new light. We are told, "In the biblical world, 'to know' had a very special and intimate meaning: 'Adam knew his wife; and she conceived, and bore Cain' and 'Cain knew his wife; and she conceived, and bore Enoch'" (Genesis 4:1, 7).[59] *The Gospel of Mary*, an apocryphal Gnostic writing, is quoted in the same paragraph, that "Surely the Savior knew her well."

From this we are expected to seriously consider that Jesus and Mary Magdalene were married. Of course, we are also expected, despite numerous unresolved additional difficulties, that Talpiot was their resting place.

Finally, the authors attempt a sincere plea to test DNA from the child-sized ossuary of "Judah, son of Jesus." Then, they claim, they could possibly determine for certain whether he was a child of two. Citing conflicts with the IAA, they conclude, "It did not seem to matter."[60] One DNA test and they suddenly had enough evidence to prove their link.

Yet too many questions remain unanswered. In a *Free Republic* article, the author notes that:

> They only did one DNA test according to the program and the book. James Cameron said on Larry King that the tests are expensive and their resources aren't unlimited. As it turns out, they chose to compare the two DNA samples that presented the least risk for their story. If they tested Jesus and Mary, his mother, and found no match, the story is over. If they test Jesus and Judah without a match, it's over. Jesus and Mara was the safest comparison because a negative leaves open the possibility for them to suggest the marriage, which is necessary for their story to work. Yet there are any number of reasons they aren't related via the same mother. The only reason to "suggest" Jesus and Mara were married is their weak speculation that this Mara is Mary Magdalene.[61]

What do others think of the DNA evidence? In a *Pulpit Magazine* blog, several experts were quoted on the subject. Their words provide the other side of the story:[62]

Dr. Carney Matheson, Lakehead University Paleo-DNA Laboratory, the one who did the DNA testing for the filmmakers:

> The only conclusions we made was that these two sets [from the "Yeshua" and "Mariamne" ossuaries] were not maternally related. To me it sounds like absolutely nothing.

Elsewhere, Matheson noted that possible relationships (which DNA cannot establish) could be:

> "...father and daughter, paternal cousins, half brother and sister (sharing the same father) or simply unrelated individuals. The media does what they want."

And elsewhere:

> There is a statement in the film that has been taken out of context. While marriage is a possibility, other relationships like father and daughter, paternal cousins, sister-in-law or indeed two unrelated individuals [are also possible]... (Discovery Channel debate with Ted Koppel which followed the documentary on Sunday night.).

Dr. Darrell Bock, Research Professor of New Testament Studies at Dallas Theological Seminary:

> "There is the DNA showing that Mariamne and Jesus DNA residue do not match. Now with how many women in Judea would Jesus' DNA not match? Even women named Mary/Mariamne? This proves nothing. ... In fact, the fact that only two boxes were tested means that we do not even know if this is a family tomb, since the two tested show no relationship. The DNA could prove the exact opposite of what is being claimed."

Dr. James White, Christian apologist, Director of Alpha and Omega Ministries:

> "One of the main 'tests' I had in mind for this book [*The Jesus Family Tomb*] when I picked it up was this: Will the book honestly discuss the limitations of mitochondrial DNA? Will they admit that such analysis can only speak to maternal relations, not to paternal relations? Will they tell us what Dr. Carney Matheson has confirmed that such a test cannot rule out that Yeshua ben Yosef was the father of Mariamne? Or will they spin the results? The answer was: spin, spin, spin.

Dr. Al Mohler, President of The Southern Baptist Theological Seminary:

> "The DNA testing is to me the most laughable aspect of all of this. I mean, frankly, there could be a thousand, thousand different explanations for whatever DNA pattern they could find."

Dr. Gary Habermas, Chair of the Department of Philosophy and Theology, Liberty University: "The ONLY THING the DNA evidence establishes positively is that this 'Jesus' and this 'Mariamene' found in the tomb are not maternally related. This hardly shows that they were probably married! So this is only a guess. She could have been married to any one of the four men, or to other family members, or she could someone's daughter. We must remember that family tombs were from extended families and were often multi—generational. So, Mariamene could have lived decades earlier or later than Jesus."

Dr. Andreas Kostenberger, professor of New Testament and Greek at Southeastern Baptist Theological Seminary, also notes a humorous thought in this very serious debate: "The claim that Mary Magdalene's bones were found in one of the ossuaries on the basis that the name 'Mariamne' (Mary) is inscribed on it is bogus; the connection drawn here is pulled completely out of thin air. [Moreover,] If you had been Jesus and (for argument's sake) had had a son, would you have named him Judas (same as Judah or Jude), like the man who betrayed you?"[63]

Interestingly, mitochondrial DNA testing is much more unreliable than nuclear DNA testing. It only allows us to discover if someone has the same mother. In fact, its accuracy has even been argued against in contemporary court cases.[64] This being the case, why would so much emphasis be placed upon this one point? Maybe it's because it makes a good story. Maybe it's because so much money was spent to provide this test. Maybe it was just the best evidence that could be presented for the documentary's viewpoint.

In the end, all that the DNA test did was prove that two people in a first century tomb were unrelated. Considering the fact that their names were written in different languages (Hebrew and Greek), this would even be expected beforehand. But to suggest anything more is merely speculation, something *The Lost Tomb of Jesus* documentary provides in abundance.

Mary, Mary, Quite Contrary: How Can We Tell Mary Is Mary Magdalene?

Mary Magdalene continues to make headline news even in the twenty-first century. Whether in *The Da Vinci Code,* in one of her numerous bestselling books, or multiple documentaries, Mary Magdalene has attained postmodern celebrity status. Unfortunately, the Mary Magdalene described for today looks little like the Mary Magdalene of the New Testament.

In an interesting interview on CNN's *Anderson Cooper 360* regarding "The Lost Tomb of Jesus" documentary, Cooper spoke with Dr. Darrell Bock of Dallas Theological Seminary to hear what the Bible says on the issue:

> COOPER: Professor Bock, as you know, this Discovery Channel documentary is claiming to have found evidence that Jesus and Mary Magdalene were husband and wife, based on DNA testing. Obviously, the evidence is pretty slim that they are pointing to.
>
> But is there anything in the Bible that actually supports the notion that these two were ever married?
>
> DARRELL BOCK: Absolutely not. There's nothing in the Bible. There are only two passages and extra biblical materials from which you have to make major inferences in order to get into the position to think about Jesus being married. So, and out of volumes of material, that's not very much.
>
> COOPER: So why do you think there's this fascination, both in *The Da Vinci Code* and now with this tomb documentary about the idea that Jesus was married?

BOCK: Well, I think for a lot of people the idea that Jesus would be married sounds, at one level, very, very human. So there's a very understandable desire to have him kind of have the full round of human experience.

But in fact, *there's absolutely no evidence for it*. And for Jews of that period who were particularly religiously dedicated, for example, the Essenes, the idea of remaining celibate in order to carry out the calling before God was common. And so it's not unusual that this would happen for someone who was as religiously dedicated as Jesus was.

The Lost Tomb of Jesus pushes the following conclusions about Mary Magdalene:

1. That she was a follower of Jesus.
2. That she was married to Jesus and had a child named Jude.
3. That she is the Mary ossuary in the Talpiot Tomb.

We'll address each of these issues regarding Mary Magdalene in investigating the facts used in this documentary. It is especially important to note that much of the documentary stands or falls on this issue, including the DNA testing, the assumptions in the statistics, and the conclusion that the Talpiot Tomb contains the family ossuaries of Jesus and his other family members.

THAT SHE WAS A FOLLOWER OF JESUS.

This first point, that Mary Magdalene was a follower of Jesus, finds ample evidence in both the New Testament and in church history. First, the New Testament identifies several Mary's, so it is important to determine which passages address her directly. The New Testament mentions six different Mary's, including:

1. Mary the mother of Jesus
2. Mary Magdalene, a women from Magdala
3. Mary, the sister of Lazarus and Martha
4. Mary of Cleophas the mother of James the less
5. Mary the mother of John Mark, a sister of Barnabas

6. Mary, a Roman Christian who is greeted by Paul in Romans 16:6

Of these six, the two most frequently mentioned are Mary the mother of Jesus and Mary Magdalene. In the New Testament, Mary Magdalene is mentioned a total of twelve times regarding eight different events, as illustrated in the following table:

Table 1. Mary Magdalene in the New Testament

Text	Occasion
Luke 8:2	Traveled as a follower of Jesus.
Matthew 27:56, Mark 15:40, John 19:25	One of the women watching Jesus at the cross.
Matthew 27:61, Mark 15:47	With the other Mary watching the burial of Jesus.
Mark 16:1	Purchased spices to use in anointing Jesus' body.
Matthew 28:1	Went with other Mary to look at the tomb.
John 20:1	Saw that stone had been rolled away.
Mark 16:9	Jesus appears to Mary Magdalene first.
Luke 24:10, John 20:10-18	Along with other women, told the apostles they had seen Jesus alive.

Mary Magdalene followed Jesus, watched him die on the cross, watched him be placed in the tomb with a stone rolled in front of it, purchased spices to anoint his body, walked to the tomb with other women, saw that the stone had been removed, saw Jesus, and told the apostles of his resurrection. Interestingly, we are told that previous to following Jesus that seven demons had been "cast out" from her, indicating her difficult past and now transformed life (Mark 16:9, Luke 8:2).

The name Mariamne is never used of Mary Magdalene in the New Testament. Rather, the Greek name Mariva or Mariavm is always used of her (the same is true of Jesus' mother). The name Mariamne, in fact, never occurs in the New Testament. The earliest possible reference found that might use this name for Mary Magdalene is Hippolytus, *Haereses* 5.7, though there is not enough information in the context to make a positive identification with Mary Magdalene.

The church father Hippolytus lived around A.D. 170-236. He says that Mary is the "apostle of the apostles," yet the version of his work that includes this phrase does not even appear until the tenth century. Even in this version, the word "apostle" is not used in the same sense as that which refers to the original twelve apostles.65 Hippolytus was writing about the women (plural) who were witnesses at the tomb. All of them, not just Mary, were apostles (plural) to the apostles. Hippolytus was not using "apostles" in the technical sense of church office. Rather, he used the everyday meaning of someone who is commissioned with a message, speaking on behalf of another. These women were apostles sent by Jesus to deliver a message to the apostles—mainly that he has risen from the dead. In that sense, Hippolytus says they were apostles to the apostles, not in the in the sense of church office.[66]

After that, the apocryphal *Acts of Philip*, from the fourth century, have this name. But that is so late that its historical credibility on other fronts is deemed worthless by most scholars.

Mary Magdalene *did* become a strong role model for the early church. As such, she received veneration in later church history, along with becoming the object of legendary stories, some of which greatly influenced the views used in the Lost Tomb of Jesus documentary.

For instance, in the *Golden Legend* (1.374-83) from the eighth century, Mary is called an "apostle to the apostles," meaning she was their leader. She was the beautiful daughter of wealthy parents and the sister of Martha and Lazarus. In another legend, she was betrothed for marriage to John the

Evangelist, but loses him when he becomes a disciple of Jesus. As an apostle, she becomes a missionary to Ephesus and then Marseilles in France, where she preaches alongside Martha and Lazarus.

Then there is the medieval myth in which she spends thirty years in Marseilles in penance as one of the seventy-two disciples who traveled to evangelize the region. In this story, she dies after a final Communion with the angels of heaven and is buried in Vezelay, later the twelfth century Basilica of la Madeliene.[67]

Other medieval creations include New Testament connections between Mary Magdalene with the story of the sinful woman in Luke 7:36-50. There, Jesus and his friends dine with a local man named Simon and other guests, who are appalled that Jesus would allow this unnamed woman to wash his feet with her tears. Another popular connection, highlighted most recently in Mel Gibson's portrayal of the scene in *The Passion of the Christ*, is made with the account in John 7:53-8:11. Despite the fact that many early manuscripts do not even contain this passage as well as the fact that the woman's name is never given, many continue to make the "woman caught in adultery" one and the same with Mary Magdalene. According to the New Testament, there is no mention of Mary Magdalene as a prostitute. The first mention of Mary as a prostitute originates from a sermon errantly delivered by Pope Gregory the Great in A.D. 591.

THAT SHE WAS MARRIED TO JESUS AND HAD A CHILD NAMED JUDE.

In the book *The Gospel of Philip* is the term "Mariamene" which some scholars think refer to Mary Magdelene. Therefore, the inscription in the tomb which uses that term has been linked to the biblical Mary Magdalene via this old document. However, the oldest copy of *The Gospel of Philip* is from the fourteenth century and is a copy of a fourth century text. How reliable is the document known as *The Gospel of Philip*? The text is generally considered to have been a late fourth or early fifth century fantasy, involving miracles and supposedly clever dialogue, which it claims caused Phillip to win many converts. So, is a phrase in a fantasy-based document evidence that Jesus married Mary Magdelene?[68] According to the filmmakers, the answer is yes.

But just what evidence do we have regarding *The Gospel of Philip*? *The Gospel of Philip* is a collection of sayings, supposedly of Jesus. It focuses a great deal on the "sacrament of marriage" as a "sacred mystery." *The Gospel of Philip* does not claim to have been written by Jesus' disciple Philip. It is titled "the Gospel according to Philip" due to Philip being the only disciple of Jesus who is named in the gospel (73:8).

The most complete manuscript of the gospel of Philip was discovered in the Nag Hammadi library in Egypt in 1945. It is written in the Coptic language and is dated to approximately the 4th century A.D. The gospel of Philip is a Gnostic gospel, presenting a Gnostic viewpoint of Jesus and His teachings. While there are a few verses in the gospel of Philip that resemble the four Biblical Gospels, a reading of the gospel of Philip will discover many irreconcilable differences and a completely different message of who Jesus was and what He came to do.

But what about the mysterious Nag Hammadi documents? Upon investigation, we find that most of these texts consist of later works termed Gnostic gospels:

> The Nag Hammadi Texts ... are named after the place they were found on the west bank of the Nile. A library was found containing forty-five texts written in the Coptic language. These were written from the early second century to the fourth century AD. Examples of texts included The Gospel of Thomas, The Gospel of Philip, The Acts of Peter and others. These texts were Gnostic in character and found in a library of Gnostic works...[69]

Gnosticism was a problem even in the first century church. The claim that such works are secret gospels can hardly withstand serious research. The church had known of these documents for centuries. Iraneaus (A.D. 130-200) and Tertullian (A.D. 160-225) mentioned the texts in their letters along with their rejection of them. These texts were never considered part of the inspired writings of the apostles.

In *The Da Vinci Code*, for instance, Teabing cites *The Gospel of Philip* as his "proof" for Christ's marriage relationship, quoting: "...the companion of the Savior is Mary Magdalene. Christ loved her more than all the disciples and used to kiss her often on her mouth. The rest of the disciples were offended by it and expressed disapproval. They said to him, 'Why do you love her more than all of us?'"[70]

The Da Vinci Code suggests this passage proves that Mary Magdalene was the companion of Jesus. It also claims that in Aramaic "companion" means "spouse." This is inaccurate if not misleading. As Dr. Paul Meier points out:

> Crucial segments of the passage Brown will cite are missing in the manuscript, since the first line actually reads: "And the companion of...Mary Magdalene...her more than the disciples...kiss her..." Yet Brown bravely translates the subject as Jesus (who, by the way, may have kissed only her hand). And "companion," Brown renders as "spouse or wife in Aramaic."[71]

The problem with the assertion in *The Da Vinci Code* is that the *Gospel of Philip* wasn't written in Aramaic, it was written in Coptic. The word "companion" is borrowed from Greek. According to New Testament scholar Ben Witherington, it most likely means "sister."[72] Within this context, it likely suggests a spiritual relationship.[73] According to Dr. Darrell Bock, New Testament research professor at Dallas Theological Seminary, the term for "companion" is not even the typical term used for wife.[74]

Can you begin to see the problems associated with such sources? The dotted sections indicate broken locations in the manuscript where it is damaged. In other words, the words inserted are the guesses of scholars. The *Gospel of Philip* never actually says Jesus was married. Worse, this source dates to about A.D. 275, *two hundred years* after the writing of the traditional gospels. Could a book written so far removed from the event suddenly announce such a profound secret not mentioned in earlier gospels? When looking at the details, the novel doesn't even include the correct original language.[75]

Some even try to argue that since it was expected of every Jewish man to marry, then surely Jesus must have married at some point. However, this argument has the following weaknesses:

1. First, several Jewish spiritual leaders remained single. The Old Testament highlights Jeremiah while the New Testament provides the example of John the Baptist.
2. Second, entire religious communities of the time included unmarried men. The Essene community in Qumran shows an early example of such a celibate lifestyle.
3. Third, Jewish leaders often granted exceptions to the general rule of marriage. It was certainly not an unchangeable requirement.

Whatever the case, even if the *Gospel of Philip* explicitly stated that Jesus was married to Mary Magdalene, that would not make the idea true. The *Gospel of Philip* was not written by the apostle Philip or anyone who had ever met Jesus. The original writing of the *Gospel of Philip* is dated to the third century A.D. at the earliest...at least 200 years after Jesus' death. The only value in studying the *Gospel of Philip* is in learning what heresies existed in the early centuries of the Christian church.[76]

The Gospel of Philip has been cited for the idea that Jesus married Mary Magdalene. Much of *The Gospel of Philip* is dedicated to a discussion of marriage as a sacred mystery, and two passages directly refer to Mary Magdalene and her close relationship with Jesus:

> There were three who always walked with the Lord: Mary, his mother, and her sister, and Magdalene, the one who was called his companion. His sister and his mother and his companion were each a Mary.

That passage is also interesting for its mention of Jesus' sister (Jesus' sisters are also mentioned in the New Testament at Mark 6:3), although the text is confusing on that point: she appears to be described first as the Virgin Mary's sister, then as the sister of Jesus, although this may be a translation problem. The other passage referring to Mary Magdalene is incomplete and was mentioned above. It is dismissed by Ian Wilson[77] who argues that it "has no special claim to an early date, and seems to be merely a Mills and Boon-style fantasy of a type not uncommon among Christian apocryphal literature of the third and fourth centuries."

According to Dr. Ben Witherington,

> "Mary Magdalene is called 'Maria' constantly in first century Christian literature, and indeed well into the second century as well. She is never called Mariamene or the like. It is anachronistic and inappropriate to bring in later Gnostic document evidence from the Acts of Philip or the Gospel of Mary, neither of which date before the end of the second century A.D. to make your case when you have perfectly good first century data to help you. In fact, in regard to the former manuscript what we have is a 14th century manuscript which is theorized to go back to the fourth century A.D. It does not identify Mariamene as Mary Magdalene, rather it identifies her as the sister of Philip the apostle. It is the unproven theory of Francis Bovon, without real supporting evidence that Mariamene refers to Mary Magdalene. There are two problems with this: 1) we have both Mary Magdalene, and Philip in the NT, and the two are never connected at all. Indeed they are from different cities it seems clear. In terms of historical methodology you cannot use later Gnostic documents filled with wild fictional accounts, indeed fairy tales, about talking animals (yes we have that in the Acts of Philip) and like and be taken seriously when you want to make historical claims on the basis of such later and non-historically oriented evidence; 2) the accounts in the Acts of Philip have Maramene evangelizing foreign countries, yet on the argument of the film producers of this Discovery Channel special, she stayed in Jerusalem and was buried there with Jesus. In other words, we have no good historical connection between the sister of Philip, and Mary Magdalene. None."[78]

The author of *Extreme Theology* presents an even stronger argument, stating,

> "The *only* way the film's producers could build their case is by setting aside the eye-witness testimony of the New Testament Gospels which never once refer to Mary Magdalene as Mariamne. They instead favor an obscure 4th

century Gnostic document called the Acts of Philip in order to make their claim that Mary Magdalene and the Mariamne of the Talpiot Tomb are one in the same.

"By doing this, the film's producers are literally expecting us to believe that a document written nearly 300 years after Jesus and Mary Magdalene walked the Earth is *more* credible and *more* accurate than the New Testament documents which were written by eye-witnesses *very* shortly after the events they record. This is absurd!

"Furthermore, if you actually take the time to read the Acts of Philip you will notice some very funny things. The first thing you'll notice is that the book itself very fanciful. The book's narrative claims that Jesus sent out a group of followers to spread his message. The followers were Philip, Bartholomew, and a woman named Mariamne who is identified as Philip's sister. Among their accomplishments was the conversion of a talking leopard, a talking goat, and the slaying of a dragon. Yes, that is right Bartholomew, Philip and Mariamne went out preaching Jesus' message to talking leopards and talking goats!

"Secondly, the Acts of Philip never even once refers to Mariamne as Mary Magdalene. Granted, some scholars speculate that Mariamne could be Mary Magdalene but the text never actually says that. Therefore, the film's producers are literally overstating the evidence supplied to us in the Acts of Philip."[79]

To get Mariamne to match Mary Magdalene rather than one of numerous other Mary's, a researcher would be required to find historical information that notes such a connection. According to one report:

> François Bovon of Harvard was brought in to make the critical link between the name Mariamne and Mary Magdalene. This link is made possible by the Acts of Philip and the Gospel of Mary Magdalene, as this is a variant Greek name for Mary.
>
> Now, in fact, things are more complicated. The inscription actually reads Mariaamnou, a diminutive of Mariamnon. It is the only inscription in Greek out

of the six found in the cave. All he did was to verify that such a link exists between the fourth century text and Mary Magdalene. The way the special used experts was to ask them to verify points of fact to lay the ground work for the speculation but did not follow up to ask them what they thought of the actual hypothesis. This was done with Frank Moore Cross of Harvard, who simply confirms the inscriptions read the now well publicized names on the ossuaries.[80]

In the end, we have no compelling reason to believe the Mariamne of the so-called Family Tomb is Mary Magdalene, a claim that stands as a key point for the entire production.

THAT SHE IS THE MARY OSSUARY IN THE TALPIOT TOMB.

On *Larry King Live*, the filmmaker of *The Lost Tomb of Jesus*, Simcha Jacobovici, noted that:

> The other thing is, the second Mary in the tomb wasn't Mary Magdalene, you know?
>
> And her name was a variant of Miriam, a Greek variant, Mariamene. So there's two Marys in the tomb, one named Maria, which is — comes down to, in the Christian tradition, the mother of Jesus; but the other one, Mariamene.
>
> They couldn't have known in 1980 that in the 1990s, the scholars — New Testament scholars at Harvard, Princeton, and so on — would conclude that Mary Magdalene's title was Mary from Magdala, the city Magdala. But her name is Mariamene. They didn't know that. So the archaeologists didn't know what the New Testament guys knew and the New Testament people didn't know what the archaeologists knew.[81]

But are Simcha's comments on the Mary inscription accurate? In an *AP* report released on the day of the documentary's showing in Israel, we find:

> But having analyzed the inscription, Pfann, who made a brief appearance in the film as an ossuary expert, published a detailed article on his university's Web site asserting that it doesn't read "Mariamene" at all.

> The inscription, Pfann said, is made up of two names inscribed by two different hands: the first, "Mariame," was inscribed in a formal Greek script, and later, when the bones of another woman were added to the box, another scribe using a different cursive script added the words "kai Mara," meaning "and Mara." Mara is a different form of the name Martha.
>
> According to Pfann's reading, the ossuary did not house the bones of "Mary the teacher," but rather of two women, "Mary and Martha."
>
> "In view of the above, there is no longer any reason to be tempted to link this ossuary...to Mary Magdalene or any other person in Biblical, non-Biblical or church tradition," Pfann wrote.[82]

Or, as Dr. Witherington has written, "There is no way Mariamenou is Mary Magdalene. No way at all."

In his words, "It cannot be stressed sufficiently that there is no evidence at all for the conjecture that Jesus married Mary Magdalene (and note that an extra-marital affair, which some postulate, though again without evidence, would not qualify Mary Magdalene to be in the tomb of Jesus' family). Similarly, there is no evidence at all that Jesus had any children. (If he really had a son named Judah, would he not be mentioned somewhere in the ancient literary evidence? He would have been a useful figure for a Gnostic wishing to claim esoteric teaching of Jesus handed down from someone close to him, but he goes unmentioned in the Gnostic Gospels that do make such claims for other figures and unmentioned also in the church fathers who relay information about Gnostic claims.)."[83]

> The inscription itself does call for careful analysis. It specifically reads in Greek, MARIAMENOUMARA. The two words Mariamenou and Mara are written consecutively with no space between. This makes it rather unlikely that two women are named here. But Rahmani takes a small stroke between the last letter of Mariamenou and the first of Mara to be a Greek letter eta (long e). He takes this to be the relative pronoun he (eta with a rough breathing), reading: 'Mariamnenou who [is also called] Mara.' (Note that this is different, it seems, from what the Discovery Channel do when they read the eta with a smooth

breathing, meaning 'or'.) There are parallels to this abbreviated way of indicating two names for the same person.

"The form of the name on the ossuary in question is Mariamenou. This is a Greek genitive case, used to indicate that the ossuary belongs to Mary (it means 'Mary's' or 'belonging to Mary'). The nominative would be Mariamenon. Mariamenon is a diminutive form, used as a form of endearment. The neuter gender is normal in diminutives used for women. But the name Mariamenon is found only here in all our evidence for ancient Jewish names. It is, of course, a specifically Greek formation, not used in Hebrew or Aramaic.

"But we must also consider the rest of this inscription. The Discovery Channel film proposes to read Mara as the Aramaic word 'the master' (as in Maranatha). But, since we know that Mara was used as an abbreviated form of Martha, in this context of names on an ossuary it is much more plausible to read it as a name. This woman had two names: Mariamenon and Mara. It could be that the latter in this case was used as an abbreviation of Mariamenou, or it could be that the woman was known by Mariamenon, treated as a Greek name, and the Aramaic name Mara, conforming to the common practice of being known by two names, Greek and Semitic.

"If the woman, for whatever reason, is given two different names on the ossuary, it is very unlikely that she would also have been known as Mariamene, even though this is the form of which Mariamenon is the diminutive. One other point can be made about Mariamenon. As a term of endearment it would be likely to have originated in the context of her family. But in that case, we probably need to envisage a family which used Greek as an ordinary language within the family. This does not mean it did not also use Aramaic, which would probably be the case if the names on the other ossuaries are those of family members closely related to Mariamenon. The family could have been bilingual even within its own orbit. Alternatively, the ossuaries in Aramaic could come from a branch of a big family or a generation of the family different from that of Mariamenon, such that their linguistic practice would be different. In any case, it is unlikely that the close family of Jesus would have spoken Greek within the family, and so it is unlikely that Mariamenon belonged to that close family circle.

"The conclusion is that the name Mariamenon is unique, the diminutive of the very rare Mariamene. Neither is related to the form Maramne, except in the sense that all derive ultimately from the name Mariam. There is no reason at all to connect the woman in this ossuary with Mary Magdalene, and in fact the name usage is decisively against such a connexion."[84]

According to the film's own documents, which are available for download from the Discovery website, the name on Mariamne's ossuary literally reads "of Mariamne who is (also called) Mara (Mara is a contraction of the name Martha)" and read the second page of the Catalogue of Jewish Ossuaries by L.Y. Rahmani. In the notes you will see what the film's own expert says that ossuary says.

One last point: the film claims that "Maraimne e Mara" means Mary the Master. But the only way they could make this claim is if they mix languages. Mara means master in Aramaic, but the ossuary inscription is written in Greek. In order for the film makers to be correct about the ossuary text reading "Mary the Master" we have to believe that the inscription although written in Greek is supposed to be understood as being half Greek and half Aramaic. This is preposterous. Since the inscription is in Greek, if it was supposed to say "Mary the Master" it would have to say "Mariamne Ho Kurios" NOT "Mariamne e Mara." No matter how you slice it, the fact remains that there is no possible way to link Mary Magdalene and Mariamne e Mara from the Talpiot tomb.[85]

Where Does the Evidence Lead Regarding the So-Called Mary Magdalene Ossuary?

The evidence suggests, in contrast with the presentation in the documentary and book, that the ossuary claimed as Mary Magdalene does not include the name of Mary Magdalene. Further, early Christian history never mentions a marriage or sexual relationship between Jesus and Mary Magdalene or Jesus with anyone else for that matter. The earliest "suggested" evidence is based on The Gospel of Philip, written over 250 years later by someone other than Philip. Even in that case, the marriage connection is based upon conjecture rather than a clear reading of the text. Though medieval and modern legends continue to promote this *Da Vinci*-like plotline, the history is completely lacking. The evidence simply isn't there.

Regarding the use of the so-called Mary Magdalene ossuary in the statistics used in the "Lost Tomb of Jesus" special, we find the need for major revisions. The problem is that both the statistician and the filmmaker argued that Mary Magdalene was the key to the tomb's identification. If she's some other woman besides Mary Magdalene, then the whole thesis is in serious jeopardy.

Mark Goodacre has commented on the statistics involved at his academic website:

> At the risk of labouring the point, let me attempt to explain my concerns by using the analogy of which the film-makers are so fond, the Beatles analogy. This analogy works by saying that if in 2,000 years a tomb was discovered in Liverpool that featured the names John, Paul and George, we would not immediately conclude that we had found the tomb of the Beatles. But if we also found so distinctive a name as Ringo, then we would be interested. Jacobovici claims that the 'Ringo' in this tomb is Mariamene, whom he interprets as Mary Magdalene and as Jesus's wife, which is problematic. What we actually have is the equivalent of a tomb with the names John, Paul, George, Martin, Alan and Ziggy. We might well say, 'Perhaps the 'Martin' is George Martin, and so this is a match!' or 'Perhaps John Lennon had a son called Ziggy we have not previously heard about' but this would be special pleading and we would rightly reject such claims. A cluster of names is only impressive when it is a cluster that is uncontaminated by non-matches and contradictory evidence.[86]

Furthermore, the film's producers contradict their own expert L.Y. Rahmani when they claim that the inscription on Mariamne's ossuary says "Mary the Master." By forcing a double meaning on the name, taking it out of context, and misidentifying the inscription, we are shown little reason to accept the theory that Mary Magdalene is buried in the Talpiot Tomb.

Who Was the Beloved Disciple?

One of the strangest interpretations presented in the Lost Tomb of Jesus documentary and *The Jesus Family Tomb* is the identification of "the Beloved Disciple" mentioned in the Gospel of John. Addressed at length in the book's conclusion, we are told, "Clearly, the Gospels harbor a deep secret. The Gospel of John, for example, purposely obscures the identity of someone who was loved by Jesus above all others: the Beloved Disciple. No one knows why this individual is identified not by name but by reference to Jesus' feelings for him."[87]

From the start, we see how personal bias skews interpretation of this issue. First, it is not clear that the Gospels "harbor a deep secret." This is an assumption of the writer. Many would argue that the Gospels were written for the everyday person. The language used was Koine Greek, the common language of the time. The content of the Gospels does contain difficult passages at times, but also frequently uses parables, or stories, to illustrate teachings.

Second, this quote assumes that the identity of the "Beloved Disciple" was hidden. This follows much of the literature promoting someone other than the apostle John as the author of his named Gospel. For instance, in the *Anchor Bible Dictionary*, a popular reference in academic circles, the entry on the issue notes:

> The supposition that the author was one and the same with the beloved disciple is often advanced as a means of insuring that the evangelist did witness Jesus' ministry. Two other passages are advanced as evidence of the same—19:35 and 21:24. But both falter under close scrutiny. 19:35 does not claim that the author was the one who witnessed the scene but only that the scene is related on the sound basis of eyewitness. 21:24 is part of the appendix of the gospel and should not be assumed to have come from the same hand as that responsible for the body of the gospel. Neither of these passages, therefore, persuades many Johannine scholars that the author claims eyewitness status.[88]

Personalizing this interpretative issue, *The Jesus Family Tomb* suggests, "At the Last Supper, in the Gospel of John, the Beloved Disciple is depicted as 'leaning against Jesus's chest.' Again, sticking to the plain meaning of the text, what does it tell us about this 'beloved' male? Unless your eating habits are very different from mine, at my dinner table only my kids cuddle with me and lean against my chest."[89]

At the Last Supper

However, this is speculative and fails to take into account both the internal and external evidence regarding traditional interpretation that the Beloved Disciple is the apostle John. A brief look at the data reveals three specific verses using this phrase. The first is in John 13, where we read:

> After he had said this, Jesus was troubled in spirit and testified, "I tell you the truth, one of you is going to betray me."
>
> His disciples stared at one another, at a loss to know which of them he meant. One of them, the disciple whom Jesus loved, was reclining next to him. Simon Peter motioned to this disciple and said, "Ask him which one he means."
>
> Leaning back against Jesus, he asked him, "Lord, who is it?"
>
> Jesus answered, "It is the one to whom I will give this piece of bread when I have dipped it in the dish." Then, dipping the piece of bread, he gave it to Judas Iscariot, son of Simon. As soon as Judas took the bread, Satan entered into him.
>
> "What you are about to do, do quickly," Jesus told him, but no one at the meal understood why Jesus said this to him. Since Judas had charge of the money, some thought Jesus was telling him to buy what was needed for the Feast, or to give something to the poor. As soon as Judas had taken the bread, he went out. And it was night (John 13:21-30).

In this context, Jesus is sharing the Passover meal with his twelve disciples on the night before his crucifixion. During their time together, Jesus announces that one of the very followers at the table will betray him. Of course, their reaction is shock. In the account, we are told they stared at Jesus and were not sure what he meant.

Peter leaned back and asked this "Beloved Disciple" to ask Jesus which of them would be the betrayer. The "Beloved Disciple" leaned back against Jesus and asked the question. While *The Jesus Family Tomb* authors would suggest this was more of a loving gesture, this was far from the case. This conversation was one of confusion, and his followers wanted to know what Jesus meant.

The scene may have looked more like a board meeting, where a staff person leans back and whispers a question to the CEO so only one person will hear instead of the entire group. Readers of this text would have traditionally considered something more along this line of thinking rather than assuming the one leaning back on Jesus must be his child.

Of course, the translation here is important as well. *The Jesus Family Tomb* authors opt for an interpretation of the King James Version language, which reads, "leaning on Jesus' bosom." This language is archaic in our time and modern translation usually read "leaning back against Jesus" such as in the NIV text quoted above. A misunderstanding of the translation here allows the authors to push a view that the early Greek readers would not have seen.

In the Garden

To provide a further example for their view, *The Jesus Family Tomb* moves to Mark's Gospel. In their interpretation, "Mark 14:51 states that when the officers of the high priest came to arrest Jesus, a 'young' lad followed them... In first-century Jewish circles, grown men did not walk around stark naked except for light linen shirts. But a boy of ten or thirteen might."[90]

Again, context is important to understand what validity this view holds. In Mark 14:43-51, we read:

> Just as he was speaking, Judas, one of the Twelve, appeared. With him was a crowd armed with swords and clubs, sent from the chief priests, the teachers of the law, and the elders.
>
> Now the betrayer had arranged a signal with them: "The one I kiss is the man; arrest him and lead him away under guard." Going at once to Jesus, Judas said, "Rabbi!" and kissed him. The men seized Jesus and arrested him. Then one of those standing near drew his sword and struck the servant of the high priest, cutting off his ear...
>
> "Am I leading a rebellion," said Jesus, "that you have come out with swords and clubs to capture me? Every day I was with you, teaching in the temple courts, and you did not arrest me. But the Scriptures must be fulfilled." Then everyone deserted him and fled...
>
> A young man, wearing nothing but a linen garment, was following Jesus. When they seized him, he fled naked, leaving his garment behind.

In this account, also recorded in the other three Gospels (Matthew 26:47-56, Luke 22:47-53, John 18:3-11), we read that Judas had arrived with an armed crowd to arrest Jesus. Judas kissed Jesus (a typical Jewish greeting) and the men "seized and arrested Jesus."

One man, a servant named Malchus, had his ear cut off by Simon Peter (see John 18:11). The man's ear was healed by Jesus according to Luke's account (22:51). Then Jesus promptly told his disciples to put away their swords and the disciples fled.

Mark makes a special note of a young man who was following Jesus with nothing but a linen garment (minus the undergarment). When this young man was seized, he fled naked. According to the *NET Bible*:

> The statement *he ran off naked* is probably a reference to Mark himself, traditionally assumed to be the author of this Gospel. Why he was wearing only

an outer garment and not the customary tunic as well is not mentioned. W. L. Lane, *Mark* (NICNT), 527-28, says that Mark probably mentioned this episode so as to make it clear that "*all* fled, leaving Jesus alone in the custody of the police."[91]

This is but one of many alternative explanations that better fit the context of the passage at hand. In another view, according to Howard Jackson's meticulous article in the *Journal of Biblical Literature*, "Clearly, given the shamefulness associated with nudity in the biblical tradition, it is not impossible that the youth's nakedness was meant to enhance the humiliating nature of his flight."[92] In this perspective, a young man fleeing without clothing marked the extreme with which Jesus' followers were willing to abandon him after experiencing an angry mob at night, along with Jesus telling them to stop when attempting to intervene with violence.

Another important note is that the phrase translated "young man" in Greek had a broad range of definition. In 1 Timothy, for instance, Paul calls Timothy a young man, though he had to have been in his early thirties by that time. From its lexical usage, it is possible that any of the eleven disciples (minus Judas) could have been the one fleeing naked. Regardless, to suggest that the individual is Jesus' son stems more from an attempt to make a connection with *The Jesus Family Tomb*'s driving theory rather than detailed research of the available information.

In fact, the discussion digresses further in *The Jesus Family Tomb* by stating:

> It appears that Mark is telling us a sad story of an unnamed boy in his linen pajamas who followed Jesus as he was being led into the night. When the soldiers tried to grab the lad by pulling on his "linen," the boy literally gave them the slip and ran away naked. Why is Mark giving us this curious detail? Obviously, it involves an important figure. So why aren't we told his name? Clearly, embedded in the text is the hint that Jesus had a son.[93]

How this is connected with the "Beloved Disciple" is clear conjecture. First, this fleeing naked youth is not called the "Beloved Disciple." Second, the suggestion that "embedded in the text is the hint that Jesus had a son," is based on speculation. As already mentioned, this "young man" could have been any age from a teenager to early thirtyies. Third, there is no mention of a name or family connection. Fourth, we are told that prior to his resurrection, that Jesus's family did not believe in him as Messiah or closely follow his ministry, with the exception of his mother Mary. Fifth, if this individual was the son of Jesus, why isn't it mentioned? Wouldn't this have been a significant fact worthy of note? Jesus was arrested and his son runs away naked? Of course! It would have been headline news in that time. The fact that a son is *not* specifically mentioned actually argues *against* the view that this is a son of Jesus. Sixth, there is the issue of the ossuary of Jude, the so-called son of Jesus and Mary Magdalene. Based on the ossuary size, their claim that he was old enough to be out at night with the disciples and Jesus may also be exaggerated.

At the Cross

Third, *The Jesus Family Tomb* brings in the scene of the cross to support the idea that Jesus had a son. Based on John 19, they suggest, "Furthermore, John records that Jesus saw his mother with the Beloved Disciple at the foot of the cross... From then on, John tells us, Mary shared the same home as the Beloved Disciple. Clearly, they're family. Most probably, grandmother and grandson."[94]

However, the context of the scene presents a different picture. John 19:25-27 records:

> Near the cross of Jesus stood his mother, his mother's sister, Mary the wife of Clopas, and Mary Magdalene. When Jesus saw his mother there, and the disciple whom he loved standing nearby, he said to his mother, "Dear woman, here is your son," and to the disciple, "Here is your mother." From that time on, this disciple took her into his home.

Notice that five people are listed in total:

1. Mary the mother of Jesus
2. Mary's sister (unnamed)
3. Mary, the wife of Clopas
4. Mary Magdalene
5. The apostle John

The text specifically states that "when Jesus saw his mother there." There is no confusion as to the identity of the person Jesus addresses. However, the authors of *The Jesus Family Tomb* suggest that Mary the mother of Jesus and Mary Magdalene may have had their names switched at this point, which would make the two people the wife and son of Jesus.[95]

Second, Jesus *has to tell* the Beloved Disciple that Mary would now be his mother in the sense of responsibility. If he was already Mary's son (or grandson), this would not have been necessary. In fact, this scene is made to explain who did care for Jesus' mother and that even at his death, Jesus was concerned for the welfare of others.

Third, we are told that from "that time on, this disciple took her into his home." This would require a man who was old enough to have his own home, meaning the Beloved Disciple could not have been ten years old as suggested in the book. Second, this home was different from Mary's home. This would most likely indicate someone outside of Jesus' current family.

James Tabor argues that the Beloved Disciple is James the brother of Jesus in his book *The Jesus Dynasty*.[96] In this situation, the same problem occurs in John 19 in instructing the Beloved Disciple, James, that Mary is his mother. The text then serves no point. Neither option works in this text.

One problem in both of these views is that the New Testament texts are taken literally in some places but not in others. It appears as if the interpreters are simply choosing which parts of the New Testament justify their view and then claim the parts that do not agree with their view are flawed. This cafeteria approach to the Gospels is inconsistent. If the scene at the cross did occur as recorded in John 19, then why is the discussion with the mother of Jesus not straightforward, but rather some sort of secret or conspiracy?

Is Judah the Beloved Disciple?

In the end, *The Jesus Family Tomb* asks if the Judah of the Talpiot Tomb is the Beloved Disciple. However, in order for this to be the case, at least the following would need to be true:

1. The Judah Ossuary would be required to hold a son old enough to have a home to care for Mary the mother of Jesus.
2. The Beloved Disciple would have to be unidentified or misidentified in the Gospels.

Regarding the first statement, that the Judah Ossuary would need to contain a body old enough to serve as a homeowner to care for Mary the mother of Jesus, we would simply need to look at the ossuary itself. If Judah is a young child, then this scenario would not fit. This does seem to be the case based on a viewing of the documentary. While precise measurements are difficult to obtain, the visual picture of the ossuary is of someone far too young to fit the Beloved Disciple presented in John's Gospel.

The second statement, that the Beloved Disciple would have to be unidentified or misidentified in the Gospels can be best determined by a study of the phrase itself. In the Gospel of John, for instance, the exact phrase "the disciple whom Jesus loved" (NIV) is used three times. Each points to one and the same person as we will see below.

Was Thomas the Twin the Beloved Disciple?

Another theory presented in *The Jesus Family Tomb* is that the disciple Thomas was the son of Jesus and the Beloved Disciple. In fact, an entire chapter of the book is dedicated to a development of the odd identification of Thomas the Twin as someone other than or in addition to the traditional identification as one of the twelve disciples of Jesus.[97] It asks questions such as whether Thomas, also known in church history as Judas Thomas Didymus, is the same as the Judas in the Talpiot Tomb. Without even a shred of evidence, the book links Jude, the half-brother of Jesus and author of the book of Jude in the New Testament, with Thomas. Then, taking the accusation step further, the authors suggest that this Judas/Thomas/Jude/Twin was a code word for a son of Jesus and one and the same as the Beloved Disciple.

In the end, they connect almost every conceivable name they wish to create a *Judas-Thomas-Jude-Son of Jesus-Beloved Disciple* all into one individual with their main evidence coming from The Gospel of Thomas written a century after the events written by someone other than Thomas! This is the most schizophrenic portion of the entire book and documentary, including three extremely common first-century names, a concocted Son of Jesus with no historical evidence, and a phrase (Beloved Disciple) whose only identity is clearly named at the end of the same gospel.

However, a brief look at the Gospel accounts of Jesus show this to be false. First, Thomas is only mentioned a total of ten times in the Gospels. Of those ten occasions, only three accounts record any information other than his name as Thomas Didymus (a word that means "twin") in a list of the twelve disciples.

The first of these three listings is found in one brief verse, John 11:16, where we find Thomas state to the rest of the disciples, "Let us also go, that we may die with him." According to the *NET Bible*, "One gets the impression from Thomas' statement 'Let us go too, so that we may die with him' that he was something of a pessimist resigned to his fate. And yet his dedicated loyalty to Jesus and his determination to accompany him at all costs was truly commendable."[98] The overall context shows that Thomas understands that Jesus has just stated that Lazarus had died and that they were to visit him in Bethany. While seemingly pessimistic, the statement is loyalist in the sense that he declares his allegiance to die with Jesus if necessary as his disciple.

The second place is in the upper room on the night of the Last Supper in John 14. Here Jesus has expressed that he will soon be leaving the disciples, but would come back for them. Thomas asks, "Lord, we don't know where you are going, so how can we know the way?" (John 14:5). The only thing revealed here is the confusion Thomas, along with the other disciples, had during this conversation with Jesus at this point. There is still here no indication of any additional information tying Thomas as a son of Jesus.

The third place Thomas speaks is in his most remembered section in which he doubts the resurrection of Jesus. When Jesus appears to his followers in John 20, Thomas was out, then refused to believe the story when the other ten disciples told him about Jesus' appearance. A week later, Jesus appears again with Thomas in the room and Thomas calls Jesus his Lord and God. There is again no evidence of anything beyond a relationship as disciple and follower. Still, who was the Beloved Disciple? If not Thomas, then who?

Who Was the Beloved Disciple?

The first occurrence of this phrase is found in John 13:23, where we find in verses 22-24:

> His disciples stared at one another, at a loss to know which of them he meant. One of them, the disciple whom Jesus loved, was reclining next to him. Simon Peter motioned to this disciple and said, "Ask him which one he means."

First, we observe that this person is considered a disciple. This would immediately narrow the number of candidates to twelve. Second, we can immediately subtract Peter, since he is asking the question, and Judas, who is the one being discussed. This leaves us with a pool of ten disciples.

The other two occurrences of the Beloved Disciple or "the disciple whom Jesus loved" are both found in John 21. The first section, John 21:1-7 reads:

> Afterward Jesus appeared again to his disciples, by the Sea of Tiberias. It happened this way: Simon Peter, Thomas (called Didymus), Nathanael from Cana in Galilee, the sons of Zebedee, and two other disciples were together. "I'm going out to fish," Simon Peter told them, and they said, "We'll go with you." So they went out and got into the boat, but that night they caught nothing.
>
> Early in the morning, Jesus stood on the shore, but the disciples did not realize that it was Jesus.
>
> He called out to them, "Friends, haven't you any fish?"
>
> "No," they answered.
>
> He said, "Throw your net on the right side of the boat and you will find some." When they did, they were unable to haul the net in because of the large number of fish.
>
> Then *the disciple whom Jesus loved* said to Peter, "It is the Lord!" As soon as Simon Peter heard him say, "It is the Lord," he wrapped his outer garment around him (for he had taken it off) and jumped into the water.

From these ten disciples, we find six (plus Peter) fishing together. The crew included Peter, Thomas, Nathanael, the sons of Zebedee (James and John), and two other unnamed disciples. At this point, we've narrowed our options to one of six men.

The second part of this chapter includes a scene in which Jesus reinstates Peter as leader of the apostles. In verses 15-25, we are first included in a conversation where Jesus asks Peter if he loves him and then challenges him to "Feed his sheep" and to "Follow me!"

In the last half of this section in verses 20-24 we read:

> Peter turned and saw that the disciple whom Jesus loved was following them. (This was the one who had leaned back against Jesus at the supper and had said, "Lord, who is going to betray you?") When Peter saw him, he asked, "Lord, what about him?"
>
> Jesus answered, "If I want him to remain alive until I return, what is that to you? You must follow me." Because of this, the rumor spread among the brothers that this disciple would not die. But Jesus did not say that he would not die; he only said, "If I want him to remain alive until I return, what is that to you?"
>
> This is the disciple who testifies to these things and who wrote them down.

Notice several key indications of who this Beloved Disciple is. First, Peter looked back and saw him, meaning he was one of the six other followers from the boat. Second, we are told this is the *same* Beloved Disciple from the Last Supper. Following the dialogue, we are given the conclusion: *the Beloved Disciple is the author of John's Gospel.*

This is the only Beloved Disciple who fits the evidence of John's Gospel. He was one of the twelve at the Last Supper, one of the brothers of Zebedee in John 21, and recognized in the early church as the author of the Gospel of John.

Evidence of Apostle John's Authorship of the Gospel of John

We can analyze the authorship of the Gospel of John through both internal and external evidence. The internal evidence has been summarized well by Westcott's concentric proofs as follows:

1. ***The Author was a Jew***: He quotes occasionally from the Hebrew text (cf. 12:40; 13:18; 19:37); he was acquainted with the Jewish feasts such as the Passover (2:13; [5:1]; 6:4; 11:55), Tabernacles (7:37), and Dedication/Hanukkah (10:22); he was acquainted with Jewish customs such as the arranging of water pots (ch. 2) and burial customs (11:38-44).
2. ***The Author was a Jew in Palestine***: He knows that Jacob's well is deep (4:11); he states that there is a descent from Canaan to Capernaum; and he distinguishes between Bethany and Bethany beyond the Jordan; in short, he is intimately acquainted with Palestinian topography.
3. ***The Author was an Eyewitness of What He Wrote***: He stated that he had beheld Christ's glory (1:14).
4. ***The Author was an Apostle***: He has an intimate knowledge of what happened among the disciples—cf. 2:11; 4:27; 6:19, and others.
5. ***The Author was the Apostle John***: He is exact in mentioning names of characters in the book. If he is so careful, why does he omit the name of John unless he is John? Further, his mention of John the Baptist merely as "John" (1:6) implies that if he is to show up in the narrative another name must be given him—such as "the beloved disciple"—or else confusion would result.[99]

The external evidence also points to genuine authorship by the apostle John. Attribution to John is found as early as Irenaeus (mid-late second century). Eusebius further reports that Irenaeus received his information from Polycarp, who was a direct disciple of the apostle John. Furthermore, all patristic writers after Irenaeus do not question this authorship, including Tertullian, Clement of Alexandria, and Origen. Further, the Muratorian Canon suggests that John was given the commission to write this gospel along with evidence from the anti-Marcionite Prologue.[100] Textually, fragments of this gospel have been found from as the early second century, indicating an early date for the gospel that would be consistent with John's authorship.

In the end, the argument that the Beloved Disciple is someone other than the apostle John must provide information that shows the inaccuracy of John's Gospel (that it is untrue in calling the author himself the Beloved Disciple) and/or that the author of John's Gospel is someone other than John the apostle. To claim that the Beloved Disciple is the son of Jesus is a gross exaggeration based on the historical and textual evidence. Yet based on one ossuary with the inscription, "Judah, son of Jesus," the filmmakers and authors suggest a connection that is outside of all reasonable historical investigation. This, without clearly suggesting the viability of other options, once again reveals the bias of the information and a clear agenda to present only the view that promotes their viewpoint.

Revising Christian Theology: What Would It Really Change?

One of the more disturbing aspects of *The Lost Tomb of Jesus* hype has been the debate surrounding the theology of Jesus' resurrection. For instance, James Tabor, a consultant to the film and head of the religion department at the University of North Carolina-Charlotte, stated in *U.S. News & World Report* that even New Testament writings open up the question to debate. The apostle Paul, for example, refers in one of his letters to two kinds of bodies, physical and spiritual. "One might affirm the Resurrection in a more spiritual way," Tabor says. At the same time, he acknowledges that "there will always be literalists who say that unless his physical body rose into the clouds, then I don't believe in Jesus."[101]

But if there were clinching proof that this was indeed the tomb of Jesus and possibly of his family, would Christianity collapse? That depends on what kind of Christian you happen to be, of course. For 2,000 years, there have been Christians who understand the Resurrection in different ways: as the resurrection of the physical body of Jesus (most orthodox Christians, whether Catholic, mainstream Protestant, or fundamentalist); as the resurrection of the spirit or soul of Jesus (many varieties of liberal Christians); or even as a symbolic event (Gnostics and various deists).

The Discovery Channel website itself even jumps into the discussion on this issue, commenting on two key theological concepts concerning the Talpiot Tomb:

> **Resurrection:** It is a matter of Christian faith that Jesus of Nazareth was resurrected from the dead three days after his crucifixion circa 30 C.E. This is a central tenet of Christian theology, repeated in all four Gospels. ***The Lost Tomb of Jesus* does not challenge this belief.** In the Gospel of Matthew (28:12) it states that a rumor was circulating in Jerusalem at the time of Jesus' crucifixion. This story holds that Jesus' body was moved by his disciples from the tomb of Joseph of Arimathea, where he was temporarily buried. Ostensibly, his remains were taken to a permanent family tomb. Though Matthew calls this

> rumor a lie circulated by the high priests, it appears in his Gospel as one of the stories surrounding Jesus' disappearance from the initial tomb where he was buried. **Even if Jesus' body was moved from one tomb to another, however, that does not mean that he could not have been resurrected from the second tomb. Belief in the resurrection is based not on which tomb he was buried in, but on alleged sightings of Jesus that occurred after his burial and documented in the Gospels.**
>
> **Ascension:** It is also a matter of Christian faith that after his resurrection, Jesus ascended to heaven. Some Christians believe that this was a *spiritual* ascension, i.e., his mortal remains were left behind. Other Christians believe that he ascended *with* his body to heaven. **If Jesus' mortal remains have been found, this would contradict the idea of a physical ascension but not the idea of a spiritual ascension. The latter is consistent with Christian theology.**[102]

Yet many disagree, and the disagreement is not coming just from Christian theologians. Consider this comment: "'That's simply not true,' said Dyer, who called the bodily resurrection of Jesus 'the theological linchpin of Christianity.'"[103] It comes from a person who claims to *not* be a Christian.

Other skeptics have also joined with their opinions on the issue. Early Christianity scholar R. Joseph Hoffmann, chair of the skeptically minded Committee for the Scientific Examination of Religion, gives the film credit for "alerting the viewing public to the fact that there are no secure conclusions" when it comes to the early history of the Christian tradition. But he charges that the film "is all about bad assumptions," beginning with the assumption that the boxes contain Jesus of Nazareth and his family.[104]

A.N. Wilson, a skeptic who "deconverted" from Christianity as a former priest, even acknowledges the problems with a spiritual view of the resurrection. In his words, "Unbelievers in the resurrection would feel that their skepticism had been justified and the vast majority of Christian believers, who profess their faith in Christ risen from the dead, would be compelled to admit their faith had been based on a mistake."[105]

From the Jewish community, voices have noted the significance of a literal physical resurrection to Christianity as well. Marc Gellman notes in *Newsweek* that, "Unlike Judaism and Islam and Hinduism and even Buddhism, which are built on God's teachings, Christianity is built both on God's teachings as well as on an historical event proving a transcendental miracle. If the Red Sea never really split, there would still be the Ten Commandments and the Torah for me. What is left of Christianity if Jesus died and then just remained dead? ... The real divide is between those who believe that Jesus rose from the dead on the third day as proof that he was indeed the Messiah sent by God, and those who do not believe this article of faith and this audacious historical claim. Ultimately this discovery must be proven a fake, or it is a big problem for Christians."[106]

But what are conservative Christians saying about the theology of this issue? On Anderson Cooper's 360 program on *CNN*, the issue was addressed with Darrell Bock. The transcripts note:

> COOPER: This documentary also says that Christianity allows for the possibility that it's Jesus' spirit that was resurrected but that the physical body didn't rise up to heaven. Does that jive with your understanding of the Bible?
>
> BOCK: Absolutely not. This is where I think we've got a case of someone who has a cultural understanding of Christianity bumping into what Christianity has historically taught.
>
> I mean, we can conceive of that kind of a resurrection, but it's a resurrection that Christianity itself never held to, and neither did Judaism, out of which Christianity was born. They didn't hold to it either.
>
> They've all—both Judaism and early Christianity believed in a physical dimension to the resurrection that allowed a person's identity to be maintained.

Dr. Darrell Bock, research professor of New Testament at Dallas Theological Seminary, also asks,

"How did his family have the time in the aftermath of his death to buy the tomb space, while also pulling off a stealing of the body and continue to preach that Jesus was raised BODILY, not merely spiritually?

"The bodily part of this resurrection is key because in Judaism when there was a belief in resurrection it was a belief in a *bodily* resurrection, a redemption that redeemed the full scope of what God had created. If one reads 2 Maccabees 7, one will see the martyrdom of the third son of seven executed who declares that they can mutilate his tongue and hands for defending the law, because God will give them back to him one day.

"To lack a bodily resurrection teaching is to teach in distinction from what the earliest church had received as a key element of the hope that Jesus left his followers, a hope that itself was rooted in Jewish precedent. Paul, our earliest witness to testify to this in writings we possess, was a former Pharisee who held to a physical resurrection as 1 Corinthians 15 also makes clear. Paul matches the Maccabean picture noted above. He explicitly denies an approach that accepts only a spiritual resurrection."[107]

What kind of body did Jesus have? "Jesus was seen in His resurrected body, which was somehow different and yet they knew it was Him. He could appear wherever and whenever He wanted, even in a locked room, or many miles away in the Galilee and likewise, He could disappear at will. Jesus talked with them, walked with them and ate with them. They touched Him and saw His scars, like Thomas who finally believed after touching His nail scarred hands and spear struck side. Jesus was seen at different times and in different places, both indoors and outdoors, on a hilltop, along a road and by the lake shore."[108]

All of this information begs the question, why can the gospels be used to prove the names in the Talpiot Tomb, but are not considered valid for the resurrection or other issues? George Guthrie, a professor of Bible at Union University said in first century Jerusalem, bodies typically were buried temporarily for a year, and the bones subsequently gathered and placed in an ossuary in the family tomb.

"The filmmakers are therefore suggesting that the body of Jesus lay decaying in a family tomb in Jerusalem at the same time the early Jerusalem church was expanding because of its belief in a resurrected Messiah," Guthrie said. "Yet, we have no evidence from any ancient document, Christian or non-Christian, that points even to rumors that the body or bones of Jesus were there in Jerusalem."

"The claim that Jesus was buried at the Talpiot tomb," Witherington said, "means Jesus' family and supporters would have had to 'turn around and preach that the tomb was empty when they actually knew where Jesus was buried—which is highly unlikely. The idea that they could get away with doing something like that, with as much attention as they had attracted in the city, is very unlikely."[109]

And what about the Gospels themselves? The gospels in the New Testament are excellently preserved historical documents that are consistent with the time, place, and culture in which they claim to describe. If Jesus did not rise from the dead, then what about the gospels accounts? Are they fakes, compilations, lies, forgeries, or legitimate and accurate historical documents?

In his book, *The Bible and Archaeology*, Sir Frederic G. Kenyon, former director and principal librarian of the British Museum, stated:

> The interval, then, between the dates of original composition and the earliest extant evidence becomes so small as to be in fact negligible, and the last foundation for any doubt that the Scriptures have come down to us substantially as they were written has now been removed. Both the authenticity and the general integrity of the books of the New Testament may be regarded as finally established.[110]

Many others have also noted the accuracy of the New Testament text. B. F. Westcott and F.J.A. Hort, the editors of *The New Testament in Original Greek*, also commented: "If comparative trivialities such as changes of order, the insertion or omission of the article with proper names, and the like are set aside, the works in our opinion still subject to doubt can hardly mount to more than a thousandth part of the whole New Testament."[111]

The late Dr. Bruce Metzger, editor of multiple editions of the Greek New Testament, wrote in *The Text of the New Testament* that, "The works of several ancient authors are preserved to us by the thinnest possible thread of transmission. In contrast with these figures of the classics, the textual critic of the New Testament is embarrassed by the wealth of his material."[112]

It is true that there are no originals left of the New Testament documents. Yet we have thousands of early manuscripts from as early as one generation after Jesus that are spread throughout the Roman Empire. The earliest dated manuscript fragments come from as early as 125 A.D., only one generation removed from the originals. Clement, writing in 95 A.D., quotes from several New Testament books, clearly indicating the existence of those writings prior to this date.[113]

According to professor Dr. Gary Habermas, there are 45 ancient sources about the life of Christ outside of the New Testament, including:

- 19 creedal statements
- 4 archaeological sources (such as stones, graves, tablets)
- 17 non-Christian, secular writings
- 5 extra-biblical Christian sources (early church fathers)

"Through this evidence we can substantiate 129 facts concerning the life, person, teachings, death, and resurrection of Jesus, plus the disciples' early message."[114] Author Josh McDowell shares many of these extra-biblical references in his online version of *A Ready Defense*.[115]

Are these eyewitness accounts contained in the gospels less valuable than names on ossuaries found in a tomb? Surely, an explanation needs to be established to account for the claims of the gospel accounts if in fact they were lies or fabrications. If the gospels are used to verify the names on the ossuaries, why are they not also used to verify that Jesus rose from the dead? There seems to be an inconsistency in using the Gospels to verify the names on the ossuaries but then deny the claim of those same Gospels concerning Jesus' resurrection. Why accept the names but reject the resurrection when both are described in the same documents? Is it because the presuppositions of those who examine the evidence do not allow for the miraculous? If that is the case, then beliefs are forced upon evidence and the evidence is interpreted in light of those beliefs.[116]

Yet those who take a symbolic view take a different view. Non-literalists view Christianity as having an intrinsic value that transcends historical details. "The Christian faith says that Jesus is with God, which is beyond proof or disproof," says John Dominic Crossan, professor emeritus of religious studies at DePaul University and author of the 2001 book, *Excavating Jesus: Beneath the Stones, Behind the Texts*. So, does the faith collapse under the weight of a supposed tomb of Jesus? "No," says Crossan. "Because the resurrection is a metaphor"—a metaphor which is the ultimate source of the staying power of Chrisitianity and the Bible. "It's the same pattern of transcendence that you get from the first pages of the Bible, all the way to the end. Historical questions do not shake the faith of us metaphorists," says Crossan. "If you wish to take the Bible literally, do," he says. "But do not tell other people who take it metaphorically that they are not true Christians."[117]

Or, as Tabor describes, while strict interpretations would conclude that his physical body vanished, others see room in the story for a remaining body. "One might affirm resurrection in a more spiritual way in which the husk of the body is left behind," James Tabor, a professor of religious studies at the University of North Carolina at Charlotte and also a consultant on the film, told the Associated Press this week.[118]

But what is the truth of such a view? Dr. Craig Evans of Arcadia Divinity School observes, "There is no indication that this tomb was ever venerated or visited by pilgrims (e.g., in contrast to the 'House of Peter' in Capernaum). Absence of such evidence argues against identifying the Talpiot Tomb as the Tomb of the Family of Jesus. It might also be added that surely Jesus' family and followers—given the remarkable circumstances of the Christian movement and its continuing growth—would not inscribe Jesus' ossuary simply as 'Jesus, son of Joseph.' We would expect 'Messiah' or the Aramaic 'Lord,' or 'Son of God.'"[119]

Gary Habermas, author of *The Historical Jesus*, agrees: "All ancient sources agree that, very soon afterwards, the burial tomb of Jesus of Nazareth was empty. The Talpiot tomb data fail to account for Jesus' resurrection appearances."[120]

From a pastoral perspective, "The idea that there was no resurrection, that Jesus did not actually rise from the dead and that his body may have remained on earth among us mortals is impossible to contemplate," says the Reverend Schenk. "The resurrection is at the core of the faith. It's the bedrock of my understanding of Christianity. Without it I'm left with an empty philosophy, which could be traded for any other philosophy."[121]

In contrast with the spiritual resurrection view espoused by the documentary and book, the resurrection has historical been seen as the number one issue for the Christian faith:

> The Resurrection of Jesus is the central fact of Christian devotion and the ground of all Christian thinking. The Resurrection was not a solitary occurrence, a prodigious miracle, but an event within a framework of Jewish history, and it brought into being a new community, the church.[122]

But the resurrection is not the only theological issue of controversy in the *Lost Tomb of Jesus* documentary and related book. Some of the other theological issues mentioned include:

- Jesus's remains found;
- Presumably only spiritual ascension, not a bodily ascension;
- Jesus being married;
- Jesus having a child;
- Mary, the mother of Jesus, not being a virgin prior to Jesus' birth;
- New tomb of Jesus ;
- Presumably, Jesus's body being moved;
- Non-biblical views of Mary Magdalene;
- Non-traditional views of "the beloved disciple" as a person other than the apostle John;
- Interpreting the apostle John and Mary mother of Jesus at the cross as different people;

- Non-historical view of "The Twin," the apostle Thomas as the child of Jesus and Mary Magdalene;
- Appeals to non-biblical books, including the Gospel of Philip, Gospel of Mary Magdalene, and Gospel of Thomas.[123]

The Lost Tomb of Jesus documentary even has the distinction of providing new interpretations nearly unknown before of classic Gospel passages. For example, one strange theory presented in the show is that John 19 presents a conversation between Jesus on the cross and his wife Mary Magdalene, with their son being the Beloved Disciple! The problem of course with this is that Jesus is addressing his own mother, Mary. John 19:26 is quite clear—Jesus saw his mother standing there, and spoke to her about the Beloved Disciple, who is certainly not his son. In John 13 and following the Beloved Disciple is portrayed as one of the adult disciples in the upper room. Not as a child. Here is but one more example of how normal interpretations of the Biblical evidence are ignored and rejected in favor of rewriting the text to support the theory, and much later non-eyewitness Gnostic evidence from the Acts of Philip is made crucial to the case, even when that evidence itself does not likely support the case at all![124]

So what should we conclude regarding how Christian theology is impacted by accusations that Jesus' tomb has been discovered? According to Justin Thacker's comments in *The Guardian*,

> "This is not a story that casts doubt on the bodily resurrection of Jesus Christ—there are simply too many problems with the evidence presented—but it is a story about the nature of theological truth claims.
>
> These truths are self-involving narratives. In contrast to most archaeological or historical discoveries, whether Jesus actually rose from the dead or not is an event that one cannot take a dispassionate view on. If he did not rise bodily then, to paraphrase St. Paul, the Christian faith is utterly pointless. If he did rise bodily, then this vindicates all that he said, and demands that we acknowledge his Lordship over us.

> A neutral stance over the bodily resurrection of Christ is not a fair-minded, rational approach; it is a mark of intellectual and personal cowardice. It is for precisely this reason that Richard Dawkins gets so irate. Even he realises that orthodox Christianity is not something one can be anodyne about.[125]

As the apostle Paul wrote, "If Christ has not been raised, our preaching is useless and so is your faith" (1 Corinthians 15:14). Christianity stands or falls on the resurrection. As I argue in my upcoming coauthored book *What's the Big Deal About Jesus?*[126] the main event of Jesus' life is his resurrection from the dead. If he didn't rise from the dead, it doesn't matter what he taught. You can forget about Jesus and Christianity.

Why? Jesus claimed to be God, God doesn't lie, and Jesus said that he would rise from the dead on the third day. If there was no resurrection of his literal, physical body from the tomb, then he is not God and Christianity is false.

But if Jesus rose from the dead? Then he *is* God. Christianity's message *is* true. It would indicate we should listen to him and not to someone else. In fact, the Christian faith has been willing to put itself on the line down through the centuries by saying, if the resurrection happened, then Christianity is true. If it didn't, then Christianity is false.

Stats About Stats: How Did They Come Up with Their Statistics?

According to the statistical information provided at the Discovery Channel's website on The Lost Tomb of Jesus,[127] we find that the calculations used in the documentary include notes that Dr. Andrey Feuerverger, professor of statistics and mathematics at the University of Toronto, has concluded a high statistical probability that the Talpiot Tomb is the Jesus Family Tomb.

In a study, Feuerverger examined the cluster of names in the tomb:

- This involved multiplying the instances that each name appeared during that time period with the instances of every other name.
- To be conservative, he then divided the number by the statistical standard of 4 (or 25%) to allow for unintentional biases in the historical sources.
- He then further divided the results by 1,000 to account for all tombs that may have existed in First Century Jerusalem.

Taking into account the chances that these names would be clustered together in a family tomb, this statistical study concludes that the probability under random chance of observing a cluster of names as compelling as this one within the given population parameters is 600 to 1, meaning that this conclusion works 599 times out of 600.

However, according to this same Discovery Channel document, this calculation only works if ALL of the following assumptions are true (note that these are *their* words):

> That 'Marianemou e Mara' (Mariamne e Mara) is a singularly highly appropriate appellation for Mary Magdalene. Note that this assumption is contentious and furthermore that this assumption drives the outcome of the computations substantially.

> That Yose/Yosa is a highly appropriate appellation for the brother of Jesus who is referred to as Joses in Mark 6:3 of the New Testament.
>
> That the Latinized version Marya (Maria) is an appropriate appellation for Mary of the New Testament.
>
> That Yose/Yosa is not the same person as the father Yosef who is referred to on the ossuary of Yeshua.

The following details also are assumed in the calculations:

- That Matia is related to the family. Since the statistician (and filmmakers?) did not know what to do with this name, it was left out completely. In other words, this calculation assumes the Matthew ossuary does not hurt the outcome of the statistics.
- This calculation is based on the assumption of 600,000 tombs in first century Palestine. However, based on the research of others, Israel may have had a population of four million during this time, a change that would greatly impact the calculations.
- This also assumes the name read "Jesus, son of Joseph," is accurate, a reading that is up for debate based on comments earlier in this book.

Thecalculation helped propel the already explosive story. "It was really the thing that began to convince us all to give this more attention," says James Tabor, chair of religious studies at the University of North Carolina, Charlotte, who advised the filmmakers and Prof. Feuerverger, and appears in the two-hour documentary.[128]

Tabo, said in an interview,

> "No one had ever contacted a statistician or a DNA person. There's a sense in which one reason he did this is that I wasn't thinking of doing this, and the DNA guy wasn't thinking about it—it almost needed a single person to say 'This is what I want to do.' Then it just began to skyrocket because Cameron came in and it became high profile and that gave us the budget. If we were just talking

about one subject, the names, then I think it would be correct that we would not say let's have a documentary on that—we'd publish first.

The publicity of it all was then picked up by Discovery, but that's their decision—they've taken a lot of heat for it. I don't want to be critical of that—I'm not paid by them in any way. I and about four other people were brought in as consultants—Shimon Gibson for archaeology, me for history, etc. Nobody was paid—they paid our expenses, but no stipends and we have no stake in the film."[129]

Dr. Mark Goodacre, associate professor of New Testament, Duke University, notes that, "This case is severely flawed. The essential problem, as I see it, is that the matches between the Talpiot tomb and the early Christian literary record are factored into the calculations in a positive way, but the non-matches are simply ignored, or treated as neutral. This will not do. ... In short, including Mariamne and leaving out Matia and Judas son of Jesus is problematic for any claim to be made about the remaining cluster. All data must be included. You cannot cherry pick or manipulate your data before doing your statistical analysis."[130]

This is one of the most exaggerated portions of the program. The individual compiling the statistics, Andrey Feuerverger, has personally gone on record to state:

> It is not in the purview of statistics to conclude whether or not this tomb site is that of the New Testament family. Any such conclusion much more rightfully belongs to the purview of biblical historical scholars who are in a much better position to assess the assumptions entering into the computations. The role of statistics here is primarily to attempt to assess the odds of an equally (or more) 'compelling' cluster of names arising purely by chance under certain random sampling assumptions and under certain historical assumptions. In this respect I now believe that I should not assert any conclusions connecting this tomb with any hypothetical one of the NT family. The interpretation of the computation should be that it is estimating the probability of there having been another family at the time whose tomb this might be, under certain specified assumptions.[131]

In the end, the stats are only as good as the assumptions used to construct them. According to a review in *The Jerusalem Post*, Dr. Stephen Pfann, who says he was consulted by Jacobovici over the "Jesus" inscription, told him he couldn't confirm it, and totally rejects the "Jesus family" claims, is particularly withering in his criticism of the statistical analysis that purports to all but definitively prove the theory. "What database serves as the basis for establishing the probability of this claim?" he asks. "There are no surviving genealogies or records of family names in Judea and Galilee to make any statement concerning frequency of various personal names in families there. Only Jesus's genealogy appears to have survived, as presented in the Gospels."[132]

Several key questions are also left unresolved in the documentary regarding the names:

1. How do they know which names were and were not common in those days? Isn't this a relevant question to ask when making statistical analysis? Joseph, Jesus, and Mary were very common names at the time. As Christianity grew, it would make sense that people would take the names of Jesus, Mary, Joseph, etc., as a sign of respect for and identification with their Christian beliefs.
2. Statistics can be manipulated. We're not suggesting that these statistics were, but there needs to be an explanation dealing with how common the names were in the culture at that time and the criteria needs to be examined.
3. Even if the statistical analysis shows the coincidence to be improbable, it still does not demonstrate that Jesus was in the ossuary. After all there are too many other questions and problems that counter that conclusion.[133]

The comments by New Testament professor Dr. Daniel Wallace are helpful at this point. He notes that, "The statistician quoted on the show (Andrey Feuerverger of Toronto University) said that it was 600:1 probability that this was the family tomb of Jesus of Nazareth. He admitted that his calculations depended entirely on the data supplied to him and the interpretations given to such data: 'The results of any such computations are highly dependent on the assumptions that enter into it."[34] But the Mariamne is problematic both because it alone is written in Greek and because that name is not found in any literature until the second century. There's also a Matia in the tomb, though it's anyone's guess as to who he is."[35]

Dr. Stephen Pfann has since responded to the documentary's statistical analysis with research of his own. As an expert on first century Palestinian tombs and professor at the University of the Holy Land, his words on the subject are worthy of note.[136]

In his words, "The starting point for the supposed scientific investigation of a tomb in Jerusalem's East Talpiot neighborhood is an amazing claim that statistically, the viewer must accept the fact that the tomb is certainly (600 to 1 probability) the tomb of Jesus of Nazareth and his family. This statement is based upon a number of fallacies and a general misuse of statistics.

First, what database serves as the basis for establishing the probability of this claim? There are no surviving genealogies or records of family names in Judea and Galilee to make any statement concerning the comparative frequency of various personal names in families there. Only Jesus' genealogy appears to have survived, as presented in the Gospels (see Matthew 1:1-17, Luke 3:23-34, together with the list of his brothers cited above). To make any statement concerning the actual identification of the family is pure speculation, since there are no other complete family lists available for comparison, and is inappropriate to describe under the rubric of "statistics."

What can a statistician justifiably say? Perhaps only that it would take another 600 tombs of similar size, form and contents to arrive at one with ossuaries bearing the identical names and numbers of this one. Even for this, there are a number of hurdles to cross.

Second, the records of who and how many individuals were actually buried in any given family tomb in first century Judea and Galilee cannot be ascertained solely on the basis of examining the extant names on the surviving ossuaries in the tomb. This is due to the following circumstances:

- Most tombs have already been visited and looted in antiquity or in recent times, leaving the record of their original contents incomplete.
- Not all ossuaries are saved during the excavations so as to be stored and registered. Oftentimes, only ossuaries with inscriptions, decorations or both are kept.
- According to L. Y. Rahmani, *A Catalogue of Jewish Ossuaries*, of 917 ossuaries in the collections of the State of Israel, only 231 (25.2%) are inscribed with names. The East Talpiot tomb is unusual in that 6 of its 9 registered ossuaries (66%) were actually inscribed with names. If all tombs contained similar percentages of inscribed bone boxes, then a comparative census between various tombs would be sensible and possible. However this is certainly far from being the case.
- Those ossuaries which bear names have often contained the remains of more than one individual. The names of these individuals will never be known. (For example, the Caiaphas' ossuary contained the remains of several individuals, including one middle aged man.)

As a result, the most one can hope to do in establishing a working database upon which to base a statistical probability is to make a general overall survey and census of inscribed ossuaries. This is a useful enterprise when utilizing the entire corpus of ossuaries to determine the proportions of names and the ethnic character of the general population. Remarkably, only 72 different Jewish names are represented among the 286 personal names found on the 231 inscribed ossuaries (bearing in mind that some ossuaries contain two or three names in the formula "x son of y")! These 72 personal names include their shortened forms and their Greek or Latin equivalents. What is the implication of this for establishing a statistical probability of occurrence?

Compared with the large pool of individual personal names in use today in North America and Europe, a very small pool of personal names was normally used when naming a child in first century Judea and Galilee. Again, remarkably, a mere 16 of the 72 personal names account for 75% of the inscribed names (214 in all). The frequency list of personal names on inscribed ossuaries is as follows:

- Salome (Shalom, Shlomzion)26
- Simon (Shim'on)26
- Mary (Miriam, Maria)20
- Joseph19
- Judas (Yehudah)18
- Lazarus (El'azar, Eli'ezer)16
- Joezer (Yeho'azar)13
- John (Yehonan)12
- Martha11
- Jesus (Yeshua')10
- Saul10
- Ananias (Hananiah)10
- Matthew (Mattitiyahu, Mattai)8
- Jonathan (Yehonatan)6
- Jacob/James (Ya'aqov)5
- Ezekias (Hezekiah)4

Total names 4x or more: 214

Other less common names:

- 3x: Amah, Hanan, Shalum, Shappira
- 2x: Azaviah, Ahai, Haniah, Hanin/Hanun, Yatira, Ezra, Qariah, Shamai, Seth

All of the names that are ascribed in the Gospels to Jesus of Nazareth's father (Joseph), mother (Mary) and brothers (Jacob/"James", Joseph/Josehs, Simon, and Judas) are found in the list of the 16 sixteen most commonly inscribed names. In fact, four of these names, Simon, Mary, Joseph and Judas are among the top five in the frequency list of names (109 of 286 names: 38% of the entire list of names).

Concerning the East Talpiot tomb, only one name among those of Jesus' brothers Joseph/Joseh, can identified on the inscribed ossuaries. All of the other siblings' names, including "James"/Jacob, are curiously lacking. Even the name Joseh is not inscribed as a "son of Joseph" or any other, that is to say, where one would expect "Joseh son of Joseph" in a purported Jesus' family tomb, one does not find it.

The names Mary (2x), Joseph/Joseh (2x), Judas and even Jesus, found in the Talpiot tomb should well be expected there (or in almost any other tomb in the area, for that matter). These are simply the most common names of the day. The only difference is that the Talpiot tomb has so many names preserved among its ossuaries! If other tombs contained so many inscribed ossuaries, the name census in most other tombs would be very much the same. This being the case, there very well could be numerous tombs which could have claim to the title "a Jesus family tomb." However in all cases, as in this, there would be no compelling reason to connect them with Jesus of Nazareth!

Witherington further comments that, "We should note that the surviving six names are only six of many more who were buried in this family tomb. There may have been as many as 35. The six people whose names we have could have belonged to as many as four different generations. This is a large family tomb, which would certainly have been used for quite some time by the same family. We should not imagine a small family group. Some members of the family of Jesus we know lived in Jerusalem for only three decades (from the death of Jesus to the execution of his brother James in 62). None of our other evidence would suggest that there were so many of them as to require a tomb of this size.

"Only three of the six named persons correspond to the names of known members of the family of Jesus: Jesus son of Joseph, Maria (Jesus' mother or his aunt, the wife of Clopas), Yose (Jesus' brother was known by this abbreviated form of the name Joseph: Mark 6:3). In a family tomb only members of the family (members by birth or, mostly in the case of women, marriage) would be interred. The fact that one of Jesus' close disciples was named Matthew has no significance at all for identifying the person in the ossuary labeled Matthew."[137]

In conclusion, the statistician who calculated the numbers used in the documentary makes possibly the best statement regarding the value of those statistics regarding the Talpiot Tomb when he writes, "It is not in the purview of statistics to conclude whether or not this tomb site is that of the New Testament family. Any such conclusion much more rightfully belongs to the purview of biblical historical scholars who are in a much better position to assess the assumptions entering into such computations... I now believe that I should not assert any conclusions connecting this tomb with any hypothetical one of the NT family."[38]

O Brother, Where Art Thou? What About the Controversial James Ossuary?

On October 21, 2002, a press conference hosted by the Discovery Channel and the Biblical Archaeology Society, anticipating a report in the Society's *Biblical Archaeology Review*, presented a small chalk ossuary that bore an inscription "James son of Joseph, Brother of Jesus."[139] Some argue that it is a modern forgery, while others, including several scholars, agree that the early inscription is authentic. In the *Lost Tomb of Jesus* broadcast, much time is invested to connect this important discovery as the lost tenth ossuary from the Talpiot Tomb. But what evidence exists to support this claim?

Dr. Ben Witherington, coauthor of the bestselling book on the James Ossuary called *The Brother of Jesus*, claims that major problems exist in connecting the James Ossuary with Talpiot. First of all, the makers of this film and book were told that the tenth ossuary found in the Talpiot tomb was not missing. It was a blank, having neither ornamentation nor inscription, and so it was not catalogued with the other nine. However, on the show, mystery is concocted when the list of the nine catalogued ossuaries is presented and it is concluded one is missing, which is false.

Witherington also claims that, "Blank ossuaries are a dime a dozen. You can buy one in the market in Jerusalem for a very reasonable price. There never was a mystery about the tenth ossuary. One was concocted for this show. It is also the case that the makers of this film were told clearly that the tenth ossuary had no inscription and in addition did not match up with the dimensions of the James ossuary, which is the focus of the book Hershel Shanks and I wrote for Harper entitled *The Brother of Jesus*."[140]

There are further problems as well in connection with the James ossuary. The claim is made in the debate follow up show that Oded Golan said that somewhere around 1980 he bought the James ossuary. This is false. Golan has consistently maintained that he bought this ossuary before the Israeli law changed in 1978. "In fact he claims to have bought it in the mid-70's and at the trial that continues in Jerusalem a 1970's era picture of him with the inscribed James ossuary was produced. The reason that the date is important is because after 1978 all such important artifacts found in Israel belong to the state of Israel. They cannot belong to a private collector like Oded Golan. The other reason that is important is it means the James ossuary could not possibly have come from the Talpiot tomb at all since it was not opened until 1980. The next feeble attempt to save the show's theory will perhaps be to claim there were other ossuaries in the Talpiot tomb that went missing from some break in. Not no. 10, but rather no 11 perhaps? Of course this will be a complete argument from silence. We do not know there were more than 10 ossuaries in that tomb ever."[141]

What evidence does the book and documentary share? After testing comparisons of three ossuaries from Talpiot with the data from the James Ossuary, the book claims:

> Combined with the New York patina-fingerprinting data, Professor Krumbein's analysis of the patina encrustations that had resided insided key letters of the "James" inscription now made a "beyond a reasonable doubt" case that the ossuraries insribed "James, son of Josephy" had once resided together inside the same tomb, for millenia.
>
> Statistically speaking, adding "James, son of Joseph" to the Talpiot cluster would essentially prove that the Talpiot tomb was the tomb of Jesus of Nazareth. "The additional probability factor that the James ossuary inscription would offer," Feuerverger had suggested, "would drive our probabilities down to *extremely* small numbers: into the one-in-thirty-thousand zone. And that would be very, very remarkable."[142]

Witherington's blog entries go so far as to share correspondence between himself and Joe Zias. Joe Zias is a fine archaeologist of long standing and good reputation. He is the person who catalogued the ten ossuaries from the Talpiot tomb, and personally catalogued the tenth ossuary. He worked with Amos Kloner as part of the team who made the original discovery.

According to Witherington, "He made crystal clear that the tenth ossuary was blank, certainly was not the James ossuary at all despite the assertions of those involved in making the Discovery Channel special. These emails have been sent along to me, and I will let them speak for themselves, except I have edited out the personal and extraneous stuff":

> Amos Kloner is right as I received and catalogued the objects, the 10th was plain and I put it out in the courtyard with all the rest of the plain ossuaries as was the standard procedure when one has little storage space available. Nothing was stolen nor missing and they were fully aware of this fact, just didn't fit in with their agenda.

Email #2:

> There was no photo of the 10th ossuary as there was no reason to photograph it, plain white ossuaries, basically once you have seen one you have seen them all. time is money and it would be a waste of time to waste resources on something which was put out in the courtyard. Remember these are large, and heavy not to forget that Kloner has the measurements. They knows this from me personally. The conspiracy idea fits in well with their agenda of hyping the film as well as his/their book.

In short, the tendentious agenda of this film becomes so very clear when confronted with the naked truth."[143]

No explanation is given as to why we have a monumental or honorific inscription on the James ossuary, but not on these other ones. "My view would be that this makes clear that the James Ossuary was not originally in the Talpiot tomb, indeed not likely there at any point."[144]

Another major source of evidence used to connect the James Ossuary to Talpiot was the chemical analysis of the patina on the James ossuary and some of the ossuaries in the Talpiot tomb match up. Again, according to Witherington, who has researched this issue in detail, "This is not actually surprising at all since you can find terra rosa in various locales in and around Jerusalem. This analysis cannot prove that these ossuaries all came from the same place or were interred in the same spot. Terra rosa is not a soil specific to the Talpiot region! And why is nothing at all mentioned about the very different sort of soil found within the James ossuary and not in these others—namely soil from Silwan, which is where the James ossuary likely came out of the earth. Silwan is indeed within sight of the temple mount. Talpiot is not. It is miles away.[145]

Eusebius, Christianity's earliest historian (fourth century), recorded that there had been a tomb of James the Just, the brother of Jesus, known in Jerusalem since New Testament times. Its location was near the Temple mount and had an honorific stele next to it. The spot was known as a pilgrimage site for many Christians.

"It was apparently a single tomb, with no other holy family members mentioned nor any other ossuaries in that place," states Dr. Witherington. "The locality and singularity of this tradition rules out a family tomb in Talpiot. Christians would not have been making pilgrimage to the tomb if they believed Jesus' bones were in it—that would have contradicted and violated their faith, but the bones of holy James were another matter. They were considered sacred relics."

This is clearly not in Talpiot; remember that to claim there is a Talpiot family tomb means that Jesus would have been buried there long before James was martyred in A.D. 62. In other words, the James tradition contradicts the Talpiot tomb both in locale and in substance. James is buried alone, in a completely different place.[146]

Yet Ted Koppel, in his interview immediately following the documentary, presented a written denial from the Suffolk Crime Lab Director asserting that he had *not* stated the James ossuary patina matched that of the Yeshua ossuary. He denied ever saying they were a match, and said he'd have to do much more comparison testing of other tombs before he could draw any conclusions.

Dr. Ben Witherington also notes in another writing that, "By all ancient accounts, the tomb of Jesus was empty—even the Jewish and Roman authorities acknowledged this. Now it takes a year for the flesh to desiccate, and then you put the man's bones in an ossuary. But Jesus' body was long gone from Joseph of Arimathea's tomb well before then. Are we really to believe it was moved to another tomb, decayed, and then was put in an ossuary? It's not likely."

"Implicitly you must accuse James, Peter and John (mentioned in Galatians 1-2 in our earliest New Testament document from 49 A.D.) of fraud and coverup. Are we really to believe that they knew Jesus didn't rise bodily from the dead but perpetrated a fraudulent religion, for which they and others were prepared to die? Did they really hide the body of Jesus in another tomb? We need to remember that the James in question is Jesus' brother, who certainly would have known about a family tomb. This frankly is impossible for me to believe."[47]

According to Joe Zias, who served as curator at the Israeli museum, "The truth of the matter is that the missing ossuary was never missing, never stolen from the IAA, nor stolen from the Talpiot tomb. Plain ossuaries which bore no inscription nor any ornaments were automatically placed in an inner courtyard in the Rockefeller Museum during my tenure at curator (1972-1997). Due to a lack of storage space this was standard operating procedure, the ossuary was given a registration number, measured and simply stored in the inner courtyard with perhaps an additional 50-100 plain ossuaries. This was personally explained to Tabor by me so as to avoid any problems of a conspiracy theory in which the plain ossuary would figure. Unfortunately, it did not fit their agenda so they artificially created a story in which a plain white ossuary, suddenly morphed into a ossuary with two rosettes on the front, traces of red paint, bearing the inscription on the back 'James son of Joseph, brother of Jesus.'"[48]

So should we give credence to the idea that the supposed James Ossuary, a first century tomb with its own story of speculation, is the missing tenth tomb of Talpiot? Based on the words of Israeli archaeologists and those most closely associated with the James Ossuary, the evidence is clearly lacking. The most the documentary could provide was a similar soil sampling, a factor that this chapter has shown as having little significance compared with the hype of the documentary. That the missing tomb disappeared is more of an issue of its insignificance than a conspiracy to link it with James, the brother of Jesus.

Parting Words: How to Handle The Jesus Family Tomb

Is this issue really that big of a deal? What if I told you that during the Easter season, a religious book...

... reached number 5 on Amazon's bestsellers booklist?

... reached number 6 on The New York Times bestseller list?

... was the second-highest search term on the internet?[149]

... was featured in a major television program viewed by over 4.19 million Americans and broadcast worldwide?[150]

... was watched by 2.2 million American adults ages 25-54 and 2.08 million American adults age 18-49?[151]

... garnered publicity in major world publications, including *People*, *The New York Times*, and *The Washington Post*?

... was produced by a major Hollywood director?

Would you consider it a big deal? Of course. Unfortunately, the big book of the Easter season 2007 is a book that claims to have discovered the tomb of Jesus and his family, arguing that he was not only married, but had a son.

But is anyone really listening? Hard statistics are difficult to track regarding the influence of a new program or book, but one study by the *Chicago Sun Times* noted that before seeing "The Lost Tomb of Jesus," 46% said the tombs are probably authentic; 48% agreed after seeing it.[152] Although a difference of two percent falls within the possible margin of error of the poll, a two percent change would be a big deal, if you are counting souls, as Christians do. Two percent of 4.19 million Americans? That's *83,800 Americans*! And this does not include viewers in Canada, Australia, Israel, and throughout Europe who watched the broadcast or those who view the DVD.

This "two-percent group" is the group most hurt by the ideas promoted in the Lost Tomb of Jesus broadcast and book. The goal of Christians should be to help those whose thinking can be easily influenced as well as the many others who lack the information to counter these ideas.

How should Christians respond to *The Jesus Family Tomb*? CARM Resources has provided an excellent article that shares mistakes we should choose not to make as Christians, along with some positive responses to this new Christian attack.[153]

Mistakes to Avoid

The initial response by a lot of Christians will be to react emotionally. When someone speaks badly about a close friend or family member, our initial response is to fight back. For instance, The Media Research Center, a conservative media group, called for the Discovery Channel not to broadcast the misleading documentary.[154] While this was not necessarily a bad choice, those who have had a more effective outreach on this issue have been those who have stepped up to address the issues presented rather than trying to deny airtime to the broadcast.

But The Media Research Center was not alone. Rev. Rob Schenk, president of the National Clergy Council, labeled Cameron and his project part of the "Anti-Christian Hollywood establishment." He urged his 90,000 constituents to boycott not only the film and the book, but also to stop watching the Discovery Channel. The Catholic League called the film a "Titanic fraud," as its president Bill Donohue said, "It's time the Discovery Channel discovered ethics and stopped with the sensationalism."[155]

As one journalist wrote, "I don't think that helps anything. Boycotting a movie or just blindly bashing it doesn't really further your cause. Christians sometimes run with emotion rather than with logic when it comes to addressing pop culture or change. Then they come off sounding like narrow-minded crazies, rather than like intelligent beings with sound beliefs."

"Instead of the reactionary, wild emotional response, choose reason. Choose to look at this film, or any other that challenges your faith, as a starting point for a discussion. Lots of people are influenced by what they see on TV. So use that interest to educate them about what you believe. Cameron is using your faith to make money; use his money to spread your faith. And do what Jesus told you to do: 'Go, teach.'"[56]

When, as some sources have claimed, a television event has cost over four million dollars to create, a boycott is highly unlikely to work. While it is important to stand for your beliefs, here are some helpful guidelines for using this attack as a way to make a positive impact:

1. **Don't make the mistake of saying that the evidence can't be true because a Hollywood movie director made the documentary.**

Just because a director makes a film claiming he has found the tomb of Jesus doesn't mean that some of the evidence isn't true. For instance, it is true that the tomb is likely first century, that the words of the inscriptions are on six of ten ossuaries, and that one of the ten ossuaries is missing. What is debated is how these facts should be handled. What options exist? We would be unreasonable in our approach to claim the entire process is trash. Our goal should be to help people sort out the facts from the fiction in order to strengthen what is true.

Christians have historically been ridiculed for separating history from faith. This does not need to be the case. Christianity can handle the disputes without losing its integrity.

2. **Don't make the mistake of saying the evidence is false because it disagrees with your beliefs.**

Beliefs don't make something true. For example, extremists who commit suicide bombing deaths believe they are pleasing Allah through their actions. That doesn't make it true. I can believe that four plus four is five, but that doesn't make it true. Christian beliefs, however, are based on evidence. The resurrection of Jesus was taught by those who personally witnessed the experience. Christian teachings have been recorded by those who spent significant time with Jesus or his apostles. When the information is evaluated, there should be nothing that conflicts with what has been historically true about Jesus and early Christianity from the New Testament.

3. **Don't make the mistake of concluding that if the evidence is verified under cross examination, that it means Christianity isn't true.**

All that *The Family Tomb of Jesus* has definitively proven is that there is a family tomb with ten discovered ossuaries, six containing common names, dated approximately first century. These facts do not hurt the New Testament teachings about Jesus and his family. In fact, when the discovery of the Talpiot Tomb was made in 1980, the archaeologists found nothing of new significance in their opinion. Not until 27 years later, during a time when our culture would be open to such programming, did this tomb become a sensationalized location.

4. **Don't blow a good opportunity to talk about Jesus.**

If nothing else, Christians must admit that this topic will generate a lot of discussion. In fact, during the heat of this debate, I performed a news search that found 500 hundred magazine and newspaper articles on the Tomb of Jesus in a three-week period. In the week leading up to the television broadcast of "The Lost Tomb of Jesus," I co-wrote an article that had over 6,500 unique visitors in less than a week. People are definitely interested in talking about and learning more about this issue.

Instead of acting like this television event and book are a plague, we can evaluate the evidence and use it as an opportunity to speak the real truth about Jesus. Paul wrote in Romans 1:16, "I am not ashamed of the gospel, because it is the power of God for the salvation of everyone who believes." If we are not ashamed of what we believe, we should also be unafraid of addressing today's contemporary issues with God's truth.

Paul displayed an example of this in Acts 17 with his approach to the citizens of Athens, Greece. In Luke's record of the event:

> While Paul was waiting for them in Athens, he was greatly distressed to see that the city was full of idols. So he reasoned in the synagogue with the Jews

and the God-fearing Greeks, as well as in the marketplace day by day with those who happened to be there. A group of Epicurean and Stoic philosophers began to dispute with him. Some of them asked, "What is this babbler trying to say?" Others remarked, "He seems to be advocating foreign gods." They said this because Paul was preaching the good news about Jesus and the resurrection. Then they took him and brought him to a meeting of the Areopagus, where they said to him, "May we know what this new teaching is that you are presenting? You are bringing some strange ideas to our ears, and we want to know what they mean." (All the Athenians and the foreigners who lived there spent their time doing nothing but talking about and listening to the latest ideas.)

Paul then stood up in the meeting of the Areopagus and said: "Men of Athens! I see that in every way you are very religious. For as I walked around and looked carefully at your objects of worship, I even found an altar with this inscription: TO AN UNKNOWN GOD. Now what you worship as something unknown I am going to proclaim to you.

"The God who made the world and everything in it is the Lord of heaven and earth and does not live in temples built by hands. And he is not served by human hands, as if he needed anything, because he himself gives all men life and breath and everything else. From one man he made every nation of men, that they should inhabit the whole earth; and he determined the times set for them and the exact places where they should live. God did this so that men would seek him and perhaps reach out for him and find him, though he is not far from each one of us. 'For in him we live and move and have our being.' As some of your own poets have said, 'We are his offspring.'

"Therefore since we are God's offspring, we should not think that the divine being is like gold or silver or stone—an image made by man's design and skill. In the past God overlooked such ignorance, but now he commands all people everywhere to repent. For he has set a day when he will judge the world with justice by the man he has appointed. He has given proof of this to all men by raising him from the dead."

> When they heard about the resurrection of the dead, some of them sneered, but others said, "We want to hear you again on this subject." At that, Paul left the Council. A few men became followers of Paul and believed (Acts 17:16-24).

Notice Paul's approach. First, he observed his surrounding culture. Rather than starting with his beliefs, he sought to find connections with what people were already doing in the community around him. Why? Because effective communication is built around connections. As Paul learned about what was important to the people of Athens, he was better able to speak to their area of interest while still teaching his beliefs about Jesus as the Christ.

Second, he made a positive appeal. Instead of beginning with criticism of the multitude of gods worshiped in Athens, Paul stated, "I see that in every way you are very religious." He wasn't agreeing with them. He was making a positive comment based on his observations. The key is that he began positive, but continued to work toward his message.

Third, he quoted from their world. He cited one of their own poets, who said, "For in him we live and move and have our being....We are his offspring" Instead of a multitude of gods to observe, our postmodern world offers a multitude of channels and choices, whether *The Family Tomb of Jesus, The Da Vinci Code, The Gospel of Judas,* to more social movements like Oprah, 24, Lost, or American Idol. As Paul did, we can choose any of these popular starting points as an opportunity to share truth about Jesus. We begin with where people are and progress toward where God desires them to be.

Fourth, Paul presented his view. He didn't just talk about society. He claimed that Jesus was the way. He was unashamed, bold, and clear about the change that was expected in following Jesus.

Finally, Paul found mixed results. The last paragraph of our passage above notes that some became disciples, some were curious and wanted to learn more, and some thought the message was nonsense. It may be encouraging to you to discover that even the apostle Paul, considered one of the world's greatest evangelists, didn't have a one hundred percent response. Likewise, as we speak truth about Jesus, we will also find some who accept our message and see positive life change, others who are curious, and others who ridicule our faith.

What Should We Say about The Lost Tomb of Jesus?

During the documentary "The Lost Tomb of Jesus," various professionals had claimed:

1. Concerning the ossuaries marked Yeshua (Jesus) and the one believed to be that of Mary Magdalene: because "the DNA did not match, the forensic archaeologist concluded that they must be husband and wife";
2. that testing showed that there was a match between the patina on the James and Yeshua` ossuaries and referred to the James ossuary as the "missing link" from the tomb of Yeshua (Jesus);
3. and that an ossuary that became missing from the tomb of Yeshua had actually been the infamous James ossuary believed to contain the remains of the brother of Yeshua.

During Ted Koppel's critique, "The Lost Tomb of Jesus—A Critical Look," Koppel revealed he had denials from these three people Simcha Jacobovici had misquoted in the documentary:

1. Koppel had a written denial from the forensic archaeologist asserting that he had NOT concluded that the remains of Yeshua and Miriamne showed they were husband and wife. In fact, he had logically stated, "you cannot genetically test for marriage."

2. Koppel had a written denial from the Suffolk Crime Lab Director asserting that he had NOT stated the James ossuary patina matched that of the Yeshua ossuary. He denied ever saying they were a match, and said he'd have to do much more comparison testing of other tombs before he could draw any conclusions.
3. Koppel had a verbal denial from Professor Amos Kloner, the archaeologist who had supervised the initial 1980 dig of the tomb of Yeshua, with whom he spoke on March 4, 2007, asserting that the ossuary that later turned up missing from the alleged Tomb of Jesus could not have been what is now known as the James ossuary. In fact he indicated there was evidence that it was not the same by saying that the now missing ossuary he had seen and photographed and catalogued in 1980 had been totally unmarked, whereas the James ossuary is marked with the name of James and a rosette.

The archaeologist William Dever summed it up when he stated on Koppel's critical analysis, *The Lost Tomb of Jesus—A Critical Look*, that Jacobovici's and Cameron's "conclusions were already drawn in the beginning" of the inquiry and that their "argument goes far beyond any reasonable interpretation."[157]

Dr. Stephen Pfann, a biblical scholar at the University of the Holy Land in Jerusalem who was interviewed in the documentary, said the film's hypothesis holds little weight. "I don't think that Christians are going to buy into this," he said. "But skeptics, in general, would like to see something that pokes holes into the story that so many people hold dear."[158]

William Dever, an expert on near eastern archaeology and anthropology, who has worked with Israeli archeologists for five decades, said specialists have known about the ossuaries for years. "The fact that it's been ignored tells you something.... It [the film] would be amusing if it didn't mislead so many people."[159]

Finally, how else could the actions of early Christians be explained without a firm belief in the literal physical resurrection of Jesus? Bestselling author Josh McDowell provides an excellent answer explaining the significance of the deaths of the earliest Christians:

> But the most telling testimony of all must be the lives of those early Christians. We must ask ourselves: What caused them to go everywhere telling the message of the risen Christ?
>
> Had there been any visible benefits accrued to them from their efforts—prestige, wealth, increased social status or material benefits—we might logically attempt to account for their actions, for their whole-hearted and total allegiance to this "risen Christ."
>
> As a reward for their efforts, however, those early Christians were beaten, stoned to death, thrown to the lions, tortured and crucified. Every conceivable method was used to stop them from talking.[160]

In his words, there was no other compelling motive for these early followers except that Jesus had physically come back to life. No other explanation can adequately account for the radical lives and sacrificial deaths by these key leaders.

According to Voice of the Martyrs, a Christian organization created to assist persecuted Christians, "Around the world today Christians are being persecuted for their faith. *More than 70 million Christians* have been martyred for their faith since 33 A.D. This year an estimated 160,000 believers will die at the hands of their oppressors and over 200 million will be persecuted, arrested, tortured, beaten or jailed."[161]

According to Dr. Craig Evans, "Why have there been thousands of books written about Jesus? Tens of thousands of articles and reviews. Hundreds of conferences. Thousands of scholars, just in the last 200 years, devoted to studying His life. What does that say about Him? I think what it says is that no matter what your assessment is, no matter which dimension or facet of His life and His person that one chooses to pursue, there's something about Him like a magnet that draws people. No matter what their persuasion is, people say, "This guy's extraordinary, nobody like this has ever lived. He's incomparable. Nobody has ever taught this way, acted this way, impressed people this way. No one has ever done these things. This is a guy I can't leave alone. I've got to study Him."[162]

Even today, those who openly investigate the information about Jesus continue to discover the big deal he was in his world, in our world today, and in their personal lives.

Jesus was one man, but he was much more than a man. Philips Brooks, the author of "O Little Town of Bethlehem," has been attributed with writing the following words which wrap up our conversation well as we reflect on the impact of Jesus in our world as the risen Christ:

> He was born in an obscure village, the child of a peasant woman. He grew up in another village, where He worked in a carpenter shop until He was thirty. Then for three years He was an itinerant preacher. He never wrote a book. He never held an office. He never had a family or owned a home. He didn't go to college. He never visited a big city. He never traveled two hundred miles from the place where he was born. He did none of the things that usually accompany greatness. He had no credentials but Himself.
>
> He was only thirty-three when the tide of public opinion turned against Him. His friends ran away. One of them denied Him. He was turned over to His enemies and went through the mockery of a trial. He was nailed to a cross between two thieves.
>
> While He was dying, His executioners gambled for His garments, the only property he had on earth. When He was dead, He was laid in a borrowed grave through the pity of a friend. Nineteen centuries have come and gone, and today He is the central figure of the human race.
>
> All the armies that ever marched, all the navies that ever sailed, all the parliaments that ever sat, all the kings that ever reigned, put together, have not affected the life of man on this earth as much as that one solitary life.

Appendix A: Additional Quotes Regarding *The Family Tomb of Jesus*

The following is a list of quotes on the various aspects of *The Jesus Family Tomb* controversy. I do not necessarily endorse what is said below. This section is designed for easy usage by those speaking, writing, blogging, or researching this topic for personal learning or communication with others. For the latest quotes and news updates on this issue, be sure to check out my blog at www.familytombofjesuscontroversy.com. Also, please send me an email via this website to let me know how this information has been helpful to you. I would enjoy hearing how you have used this resource.

David Letterman jokes,

> "James Cameron thinks that he found the tomb of Jesus Christ. To me, that's very interesting. Who would have guessed that they'd find Jesus before bin Laden?"

The show-business bible ***Variety*** reported:

> "The overall rating for the show was 3.21 or 4.1 million people. The late night encore drew another 796,000. The rating for the Koppel show afterwards was 2.1, holding on to 2/3 of the audience. This is triple the normal ratings for Discovery programs at that slot. Discovery also scored some of its best numbers ever with the special among adults 25-54 (its demo target), with 2.2 million, and 18-49, with 2.08 million." (www.variety.com)

Evangelical scholar Darrell Bock calls Cameron's doc the recycling of the story of the "James burial box story with a little of the Da Vinci Code mixed in."[63]

Bock wants to acknowledge that the documentary is a well-done detective story with high production values that does a nice job showing what the archaeological process is like.[164]

"Hopefully people in our society can tell the difference between hype coming out of Hollywood and what is coming out of Jerusalem," Bock says.[165]

"In 1996, when the BBC aired a short documentary on the same subject, archaeologists challenged the claims. Amos Kloner, the first archaeologist to examine the site, said the idea [of the tomb being that of Jesus] fails to hold up by archaeological standards but makes for profitable television....It was an ordinary middle-class Jerusalem burial cave...The names on the caskets are the most common names found among Jews at the time...The cave, it [Kloner's report] said, was probably in use by three or four generations of Jews from the beginning of the Common Era. It was disturbed in antiquity, and vandalized. The names on the boxes were common in the first century (25 percent of women in Jerusalem, for example, were called Miriam or a derivative)."[166]

"The claim that the burial site [of Jesus] has been found is not based on any proof, and is only an attempt to sell," says **Israeli archeologist Professor Amos Kloner.**" A similar film was released 11 years ago, and Kloner said that this current film was merely a renewed effort to create controversy in the Christian world in order to make a bigger profit. He added, "I refute all their claims and efforts to waken a renewed interest in the findings. With all due respect, they are not archeologists."[167]

"I would like more information. I remain skeptical," said the **archaeologist, Shimon Gibson, a senior fellow at the W. F. Albright Institute of Archaeological Research in Jerusalem,** in an interview after the news conference.

Lawrence E. Stager, the Dorot professor of archaeology of Israel at Harvard, in a telephone interview. "One of the problems is there are so many biblically illiterate people around the world that they don't know what is real judicious assessment and what is what some of us in the field call 'fantastic archaeology.' "[168]

"A lot of conservative, orthodox and moderate Christians are going to be upset by the recklessness of this," **said Ben Witherington, a Bible scholar at Asbury Theological Seminary in Wilmore, Ky.** "Of course, we want to know more about Jesus, but please don't insult our intelligence by giving us this sort of stuff. It's going to get a lot of Christians with their knickers in a knot unnecessarily."[69]

"If this were about Islam—let's put aside the fact that it's all made up. But if there were about Islam, even if it were true, James Cameron would be in hiding for at least a good ten years." –**Rich Lowery, *Fox News*, March 3, 2007**

"The much-ballyhooed *Lost Tomb of Jesus* didn't prove much of anything...well, except that attempts to disprove Scripture are deemed more newsworthy than discoveries that support biblical accounts."— **Michael Medved, *USA Today*, March 12, 2007.**

Appendix B: Nine Facts That Disapprove the Discovery Channel's The Lost Tomb of Jesus

By Dr. John Ankerberg and Dillon Burroughs[170]

On February 26, 2007, filmmakers and researchers unveiled two ancient stone boxes they claim may have once contained the remains of Jesus and Mary Magdalene. On Sunday, March 4, 2007, "The Lost Tomb of Jesus," produced by Oscar-winning director James Cameron aired nationwide on the Discovery Channel. A related book by Simcha and Charles Pellegrino entitled *The Jesus Family Tomb: The Discovery, the Investigation, and the Evidence That Could Change History* (Harper Collins) released the day of the press conference to coordinate with the special.

These researchers argue that 10 small caskets discovered in 1980 in a Jerusalem suburb may have held the bones of Jesus and his family. They even claim that one of the caskets bears the title, "Judah, son of Jesus," hinting that Jesus may have had a son. But what truth can be found in this story?

The truth is that several unsupportable assumptions have been made to provide maximum hype for the book and television event. In an effort to bring out facts which disprove the major assumptions of the film and the book, we have provided the following nine facts that disprove *The Family Tomb of Jesus* with the help of some of our friends who serve as professors and experts on Christianity in today's universities and graduate institutions.

1. The Jesus Family Tomb Would Not Have Been in Jerusalem, but Nazareth.

Dr. Darrell Bock, research professor of New Testament at Dallas Theological Seminary, asks, "How did his family have the time in the aftermath of his death to buy the tomb space, while also pulling off a stealing of the body and continue to preach that Jesus was raised BODILY, not merely spiritually?

"The bodily part of this resurrection is key because in Judaism when there was a belief in resurrection it was a belief in a *bodily* resurrection, a redemption that redeemed the full scope of what God had created. If one reads 2 Maccabees 7, one will see the martyrdom of the third son of seven executed who declares that they can mutilate his tongue and hands for defending the law, because God will give them back to him one day.

"To lack a bodily resurrection teaching is to teach in distinction from what the earliest church had received as a key element of the hope that Jesus left his followers, a hope that itself was rooted in Jewish precedent. Paul, our earliest witness to testify to this in writings we possess, was a former Pharisee who held to a physical resurrection as 1 Corinthians 15 also makes clear. Paul matches the Maccabean picture noted above. He explicitly denies an approach that accepts only a spiritual resurrection."[171]

2. If This Is the Family Tomb of Jesus, Why Does It Contain so Many Non-Family Members?

Jesus was born in Bethlehem and his family lived in Nazareth. It would be strange enough for his family to be buried together in Jerusalem. Even stranger, why would the family tomb include several non-family members? There is not a shred of historical evidence to account for this inconsistency.

On the contrary, the Israeli archeologist who actually discovered the ancient burial caves 27 years ago says there is absolutely no proof to Cameron's outlandish claims. What's more, the archeologist says that Cameron and his team are merely trying to profit by attacking a central tenet of the Christian faith that Jesus was raised from the dead on the third day and that his body has never been discovered.

"The claim that the burial site [of Jesus] has been found is not based on any proof, and is only an attempt to sell," says Israeli archeologist Professor Amos Kloner." A similar film was released 11 years ago, and Kloner said that this current film was merely a renewed effort to create controversy in the Christian world in order to make a bigger profit. He added, "I refute all their claims and efforts to waken a renewed interest in the findings. With all due respect, they are not archeologists."[172]

3. The Statistical Analysis Concerning Jesus Is Highly Exaggerated. The Name "Jesus" Was a Popular Name in the First Century. It Has Been Found in 99 Other Tombs and on 22 Other Ossuaries.

The name Jesus was a popular first century name, discovered on 121 other tombs and ossuaries during this time period. According to the details in a famous catalogue of ossuary names that has been out since 2002 with the information known about this locale since c. 1980, we find:

Out of a total number of 2,625 males, these are the figures for the ten most popular male names among Palestinian Jews. The first figure is the total number of occurrences, while the second is the number of occurrences specifically on ossuaries.

1	Simon/Simeon	243	59
2	Joseph	218	45
3	Eleazar 1	66	29
4	Judah	164	44
5	John/Yohanan	122	25
6	Jesus	99	22
7	Hananiah	82	18
8	Jonathan	71	14
9	Matthew	62	17
10	Manaen/Menahem	42	4

[173]

This indicates that of all existing tombs and ossuaries of the period, that there is nearly a 1 in 20 (4.6%) chance that any male tomb would have the name Jesus on it. Yet according to the film's statistics, the evidence is 600 to 1 in favor of their story being true.

This is one of the most exaggerated portions of the program. The individual compiling the statistics, Andrey Feuerverger, has gone on record to state:

> It is not in the purview of statistics to conclude whether or not this tombsite is that of the New Testament family. Any such conclusion much more rightfully belongs to the purview of biblical historical scholars who are in a much better position to assess the assumptions entering into the computations. The role of statistics here is primarily to attempt to assess the odds of an equally (or more) 'compelling' cluster of names arising purely by chance under certain random sampling assumptions and under certain historical assumptions. In this respect I now believe that I should not assert any conclusions connecting this tomb with any hypothetical one of the NT family. The interpretation of the computation should be that it is estimating the probability of there having been another family at the time whose tomb this might be, under certain specified assumptions.[174]

In the end, the stats are only as good as the assumptions used to construct them.

4. The Statistics Are Also Distorted regarding Mary of Magdalene.

The name Mariamne, a variation of Maria, was one of the most common names of the time. According to the details on names provided by Prof Richard Bauckham of St. Andrews and sourced in a famous catalogue of ossuary names that has been out since 2002 with the information known about this locale since c. 1980, we find:

For women, we have a total of 328 occurrences (women's names are much less often recorded than men's), and figures for the 4 most popular names are thus:

| 1 | Mary/Mariamne | 70 | 42 |

2	Salome	58	41
3	Shelamzion	24	19
4	Martha	20	17[175]

The true statistics reveal that Mary was the most common name on tombs during this time period. 21% of Jewish women were called Mariamne (Mary). This is hardly strong evidence suggesting Mary as *the* Mary Magdalene of the New Testament.

5. The DNA Evidence Is Irrelevant and Untrustworthy.

In the film, there is a DNA test showing that Mariamne and Jesus' DNA residues do not match. Based on that one shred of evidence, the researchers claim the couple was married and that this couple must be Jesus and Mary Magdalene. With how many women in Judea would Jesus' DNA not match? Even women named Mariamne? This proves nothing. It only states the obvious, that the two were not related, nothing more. Even this DNA evidence is scientifically shaky.

Dr. Jim Tabor, a professor involved in the special, answered in an interview, "No one had ever contacted a statistician or a DNA person. There's a sense in which one reason he did this is that I wasn't thinking of doing this, and the DNA guy wasn't thinking about it—it almost needed a single person to say 'This is what I want to do.' Then it just began to skyrocket because Cameron came in and it became high profile and that gave us the budget. If we were just talking about one subject, the names, then I think it would be correct that we would not say let's have a documentary on that—we'd publish first.

The publicity of it all was then picked up by Discovery, but that's their decision—they've taken a lot of heat for it. I don't want to be critical of that—I'm not paid by them in any way. I and about four other people were brought in as consultants—Shimon Gibson for archaeolgoy, me for history, etc. Nobody was paid—they paid our expenses, but no stipends and we have no stake in the film."[176]

According to Dr. Witherington, "There is no independent DNA control sample to compare to what was garnered from the bones in this tomb. By this I mean that the most the DNA evidence can show is that several of these folks are inter-related. Big deal. We would need an independent control sample from some member of Jesus' family to confirm that these were members of Jesus' family. We do not have that at all. In addition mitochondrial DNA does not reveal genetic coding or XY chromosome make up anyway. They would need nuclear DNA for that in any case. So the DNA stuff is probably thrown in to make this look more like a real scientific fact."[177]

6. There Is No Historical Evidence That Jesus Was Ever Married or Had a Child.

The argument that Jesus was married or had a child comes solely from silence. No New Testament document speaks of such relationships, nor do Christian or secular writings from the early centuries of Christianity. The closest document is the apocryphal Gospel of Philip, written approximately 275 A.D., written neither by the apostle nor in the time period of the New Testament. As our book *The Da Vinci Code Controversy*[178] notes, even the passage used to suggest a married Jesus is used grossly out of context.

7. There Is No Historical Evidence That Connects Mariamne and Mary Magdalene.

To get Mariamne to match Mary Magdalene rather than one of numerous other Mary's, a researcher would be required to find historical information that notes such a connection. According to one report:

> François Bovon of Harvard was brought in to make the critical link between the name Mariamne and Mary Magdalene. This link is made possible by the Acts of Philip and the Gospel of Mary Magdalene, as this is a variant Greek name for Mary.
>
> Now, in fact, things are more complicated. The inscription actually reads Mariaamnou, a diminutive of Mariamnon. It is the only inscription in Greek out of the six found in the cave. All he did was to verify that such a link exists between the fourth century text and Mary Magdalene. The way the special used

experts was to ask them to verify points of fact to lay the ground work for the speculation but did not follow up to ask them what they thought of the actual hypothesis. This was done with Frank Moore Cross of Harvard, who simply confirms the inscriptions read the now well publicized names on the ossuaries.[179]

In the end, we have no compelling reason to believe the Mariamne of the so-called Family Tomb is Mary Magdalene, a claim that stands as a key point for the entire production.

8. The Trouble with James, the Brother of Jesus, Is History Says He Was Buried Alone in Another Tomb.

Eusebius, Christianity's earliest historian (fourth century), recorded that there had been a tomb of James the Just, the brother of Jesus, known in Jerusalem since New Testament times. Its location was near the Temple mount and had an honoric stele next to it. The spot was known as a pilgrimage site for many Christians.

"It was apparently a single tomb, with no other holy family members mentioned nor any other ossuaries in that place," states Dr. Witherington. "The locality and singularity of this tradition rules out a family tomb in Talpiot. Christians would not have been making pilgrimage to the tomb if they believed Jesus' bones were in it—that would have contradicted and violated their faith, but the bones of holy James were another matter. They were consider sacred relics."

This is clearly not in Talpiot, and remember to claim there is a Talpiot family tomb means that Jesus would have been buried there long before James was martyred in A.D. 62. In other words, the James tradition contradicts the Talpiot tomb both in locale and in substance. James is buried alone, in a completely different place.

9. There Is Multiple Historical Attestation That Both Christians and Non-Christians Knew Where the Tomb of Jesus Was, and That It Was Found Empty on the Third Day.

Dr. Ben Witherington, professor of New Testament at Asbury Seminary and author of *What Have They Done with Jesus?*, notes: "By all ancient accounts, the tomb of Jesus was empty--even the Jewish and Roman authorities acknowledged this. Now it takes a year for the flesh to desiccate, and then you put the man's bones in an ossuary. But Jesus' body was long gone from Joseph of Arimathea's tomb well before then. Are we really to believe it was moved to another tomb, decayed, and then was put in an ossuary? Its not likely.

"Implicitly you must accuse James, Peter and John (mentioned in Galatians 1-2 in our earliest New Testament document from 49 A.D.) of fraud and coverup. Are we really to believe that they knew Jesus didn't rise bodily from the dead but perpetrated a fraudulent religion, for which they and others were prepared to die? Did they really hide the body of Jesus in another tomb? We need to remember that the James in question is Jesus' brother, who certainly would have known about a family tomb. This frankly is impossible for me to believe."[180]

Dr. Stephen Pfann, a biblical scholar at the University of the Holy Land in Jerusalem who was interviewed in the documentary, said the film's hypothesis holds little weight.

"I don't think that Christians are going to buy into this," he said. "But skeptics, in general, would like to see something that pokes holes into the story that so many people hold dear."

Dr. Pfann is even unsure that the name "Jesus" on the caskets was read correctly. He thinks it's more likely the name "Hanun." Ancient Semitic script is notoriously difficult to decipher.[181]

William Dever, an expert on near eastern archaeology and anthropology, who has worked with Israeli archeologists for five decades, said specialists have known about the ossuaries for years. "The fact that it's been ignored tells you something.... It [the film] would be amusing if it didn't mislead so many people."[182]

Should we be concerned about *The Lost Tomb of Jesus*? Yes. As Christians, we should be bothered that others would speak of the Jesus we worship as anything less than God's divine Son. But should we be worried?

No. The evidence fails to prove anything other than the fact that controversy about Jesus continues to draw attention.

Our challenge should be to know the truth of God's Word and to continue to communicate it to others through our actions and words. As Dr. Bock noted, "Hopefully our times have not slid to the point where we can no longer tell the difference between Jerusalem and Hollywood."[183]

Appendix C: Would The Followers of Jesus Have Taken His Body?

> "Conflicting traditions [to the empty tomb story] nowhere appear, even in Jewish polemic."
>
> —-Dr. William Lane Craig[184]
>
> "[The resurrection story] could not have been maintained in Jerusalem for a single day, for a single hour, if the emptiness of the tomb had not been established…"
>
> -Dr. Paul Althaus [185]

The empty tomb of Jesus is a fact that almost every scholar agrees upon. The disagreement revolves around what happened to the body.

All of the early sources report that Jesus' tomb was found empty, first by women, then by his disciples, and finally, by the Jewish leaders themselves. According to Dr. William Lane Craig shared that, "Today, the majority of scholars who have written on this subject agree that the tomb of Jesus was probably found empty by a group of his female followers early on Sunday morning. That represents the historical core of the empty tomb narrative as we find it in Mark."[186]

According to Dr. Gary Habermas, "The empty tomb is preached very early. You have Paul in 1 Corinthians 15 saying Jesus died, he was buried, and what went down is what came out, and what came out is what appeared. 1 Corinthians is already early, about 25 years after the cross. But then the creedal passage that he reports from 1 Corinthians 15 is earlier still. In Galatians, Paul has apostolic confirmation of his message about the resurrection events. These come from Peter and James in Galatians 1 and from Peter, James, and John in Galatians 2. This testimony was given to Paul *within five years of Jesus' resurrection* from those preaching since day one. So you have this intricate, interwoven, and accredited eyewitness messenger with an early book, with an even earlier creed. Ultimately, it's teaching our fact here in question—the empty tomb."[187]

Yet the Tomb of Jesus television program and related book claim that the disciples would have stolen the body before the arrival of the Roman soldiers to the tomb, reburied it, then placed his bones in the Talpiot tomb approximately a year later. For this to be true, the disciples would have been preaching the physical resurrection of Jesus to thousands at the same time they were burying his bones in an ossuary. Such a contradictory response seems incapable of these early followers, most of whom also died for their belief in the risen Jesus.

Asking the Tough Questions

In addition to the supporting historical sources by the followers of Jesus, we find that the Jewish leadership confirmed the early story of the empty tomb of Jesus. They simply handled it differently, suggesting that Jesus' body had been stolen (according to Matthew 28:11-15). The most common alternatives today continue to suggest some form of Jesus' followers removing his body and then announcing he was alive again.

Questioning the Disciples Concerning the Empty Tomb

If the followers of Jesus did remove him from his burial site, several questions would have required a credible answer. We'll consider four of the most vital aspects the followers of Jesus would have required to steal his dead body and proclaim Jesus had come back to life from the dead.

DID THEY HAVE A MOTIVE?

The friends and followers of Jesus taught that he had come back to life. Were they lying? If so, what would be their motivation? Was dissatisfaction with the Roman government enough? Not likely.

Jesus, according to his followers, modeled values of love, truth, and selfless living. Would it make sense for his closest associates to completely contradict their leader? According to one article on the subject:

> At best all anyone can do is guess about what the disciples *may* have been thinking or what *might* have motivated them to devise an elaborate deception. Guessing is all that can be done. But we would need to ask if any proposed motives of the disciples could be harmonized with the facts of their preaching and teaching about truth, long-suffering, patience, kindness, and love. No one can read their hearts or their minds and insert into a scenario 2,000 years old the motivations of people long gone. It is best to simply let the facts speak for themselves. They lived, suffered, proclaimed, and died for the truth of the resurrection.[188]

Regardless of what their motive was to teach about a risen Jesus, we can see that such a change would be in complete contrast with what Jesus had taught them over the previous three years. Yet their teaching had tremendous impact.

Even according to the best of today's research, the most likely historical scenario is that the tomb was empty. The question at hand among scholars today is: how did it happen?

DID THEY HAVE A PLAN?

No matter what theory we believe, we would all likely agree that Jesus' followers would have required some kind of plan to pull off an operation for stealing the body of Jesus. Why? According to history, the tomb was guarded by a group of Roman soldiers.

If they were to accomplish such a task, they would have to bribe or kill the guards, move the stone, and then move the body to another location. This would certainly require several people.

And the consequences? If caught, those involved would be killed in the process. If captured, they might suffer the same type of crucifixion as Jesus. Does this match the profiles of those disheartened followers who witnessed his brutal death?

In contrast with the highly-organized efforts required to steal the body of Jesus, his friends were behind locked doors, fearful for their own lives. They certainly continued to mourn the death of Jesus as well, as we discover from the women who left the home to visit the tomb on Sunday morning, just after the Sabbath rest.

But suppose for a moment Jesus' followers did obtain the body. Certainly they would need to dispose of the body in some method to prevent someone from finding his corpse as evidence against them. Would they burn it? Not if they observed Jewish law. Would they rebury it? Certainly, Jewish custom required this, but this would mean that men who had given up their careers and social status to follow a man who taught honesty and integrity were now rebels of both Roman and Jewish laws. The scenario doesn't fit.

Consider this thought: What do you suppose would happen if Jesus' followers had stolen his body yet continued to announce Jesus was alive? First, there would be persecution from Jewish leaders. In fact, this did occur. Ten of the eleven remaining disciples died as martyrs for their faith. The only exception was John, who was banished to the Island of Patmos near the end of his life. Usually, if deception is involved, at least one person would "crack" in the process. And history would certainly have recorded it.

DID THEY HAVE THE RESOURCES?

Another factor involved is to consider whether the remaining followers of Jesus would have had the resources to obtain Jesus' body. The options were to either obtain the weapons to overpower the guards or to bribe the guards through financial gain. Both options have severe weaknesses.

Consider the idea that Jesus' followers would gather weapons and take down a group of Roman guards. The night of Jesus' arrest, he asked his disciples if they had *any* weapons. They found two. Two weapons for twelve disciples and Jesus. Even those they had included only two short swords, nothing against a battalion of armed troops.

Most of Jesus' disciples were fisherman by trade. They were not trained in martial arts or the modern weaponry of the day. They did not have backgrounds as soldiers, except possibly Simon the Zealot. To obtain the weapons they would need would require makinng them (highly unlikely), or buying them.

Speaking of buying, what about the idea of Jesus' followers paying off the guards for his body? How likely would this option have been? There are a couple of ways to discuss this question. First, where would Jesus' followers obtain a large sum of money within three days of his death? The only wealthy ones among them were Joseph of Arimathea who had provided the tomb, and Nicodemus who assisted in burying Jesus. Joseph, a member of the Jewish court that had condemned Jesus, had probably already risked his reputation to ask for the body. The chances of him stealing the body from his own tomb three days later? Very slim.

Second, even if his followers somehow obtained a windfall of money to pay off the guards, would the guards have taken it? Consider the consequences. If Roman soldiers had lost the body, they would have paid for it with their lives. To phrase it in our terms, would you rather have ten million dollars and die tomorrow or no money and enjoy the rest of your life? To the Roman soldiers, this was the predicament.

The New Testament actually records two examples of this custom. In Acts 16:25-30 when Paul was in prison, there was an earthquake that opened the cell doors that would have allowed the prisoners to escape. When the officer in charge saw this he prepared to commit suicide. Why? He knew his life was about to be ended if his prisoners escaped. In Acts 12:18-19, we find Peter in prison for his faith. In this episode we read that Herod specifically ordered the guards to be executed if Peter escaped.

Interestingly, in the gospel accounts, the *Jewish religious leaders* paid money to the guards to say that the disciples had stolen the body *after* the occurrence. We are told:

> Now while they were on their way, behold, some of the guard came into the city and reported to the chief priests all that had happened. And when they had assembled with the elders and counseled together, they gave a large sum of money to the soldiers, and said, "You are to say, 'His disciples came by night

and stole Him away while we were asleep.' And if this should come to the governor's ears, we will win him over and keep you out of trouble." And they took the money and did as they had been instructed; and this story was widely spread among the Jews, and is to this day.[189]

But as mentioned above, these soldiers were probably soon executed once their leaders discovered the news of the empty tomb. We find that according to what history records, the tomb was empty and the soldiers did pay for it with their lives.

DID THEY HAVE THE CONNECTIONS?

By "connections" I mean, did they have influence over enough people to encourage hundreds of people to lie about seeing Jesus alive? How could they have been able to convince so many to speak out about a person who had just been put to death by the government? Their jobs, social status, and families would all be at stake.

Lastly, consider the sheer numbers. In 1 Corinthians 15, the apostle Paul wrote just over twenty years after the events that over 500 people had seen Jesus alive after his resurrection, most of whom were still alive at the time of Paul's writing. 500 people influenced by a handful of men to lie about such a well-known event? Extremely unlikely. If so, at this level of probability we're looking at theories requiring a tremendous jump of faith. This being the situation, we are left to choose the most likely option: that Jesus really did rise from the dead.

Jesus was not MIA. His body was buried, guarded, and yet disappeared. The historical evidence shows that Jesus was crucified on a cross, his body was laid in a tomb cut out of solid rock, and three days later, that tomb was found empty. If his body had not been removed by his disciples and the soldiers did not do it, then what happened? The traditional supernatural belief that Jesus' body physically came back to life is the only credible answer left.

References

[1] Paul Maier, *A Skeleton in God's Closet*, (Nashville, TN: Westbow, 1994).

[2] Simcha Jacobovici and Charles Pellegrino, The Jesus Family Tomb: the Discovery, the Investigation, and the Efvidence That Could Change History, (San Francisco, CA: Harper San Francisco, 2007).

[3] Glenna Whitley, "Jesus Junk," *The Dallas Observer*, March 1, 2007. Accessed at http://www.dallasobserver.com/2007-03-01/news/jesus-junk/1.

[4] "Archaeologist Disputes Claims in James Cameron's "The Lost Tomb of Christ," *ABC News*, February 26, 2007.

[5] Bess Twiston Davies, "Tomb Doubts," *The Times* (London), March 3, 2007, p. 71.

[6] Although this percentage is actually higher than what others note as we will see later in this book.

[7] "Archaeologist Disputes Claims in James Cameron's "The Lost Tomb of Christ," *ABC News*, February 26, 2007.

[8] Alan Cooperman, "'Lost Tomb of Jesus' Claim Called A Stunt," *Washington Post*, February 28, 2007. Accessed at http://www.washingtonpost.com/wp-dyn/content/article/2007/02/26/AR2007022600442.html.

[9] Alan Cooperman, "'Lost Tomb of Jesus' Claim Called A Stunt," *Washington Post*, February 28, 2007. Accessed at http://www.washingtonpost.com/wp-dyn/content/article/2007/02/26/AR2007022600442.html.

[10] "Jesus' Tomb—Pt. 2: Can Christ's Body Be Discovered?" *World News Desk*, March 9, 2007. Accessed at http://www.realtruth.org/news/070309-002-religion.html.

[11] "The Lost Tomb of Jesus? Religious Scholar Provides Insight on the Controversy," *Science Daily*, February 28, 2007. Accessed at http://www.sciencedaily.com/releases/2007/02/070228135009.htm.

[12] Laurie Goodstein," *The New York Times*, February 27, 2007. Accessed at http://www.nytimes.com/2007/02/27/us/27jesus.html?ex=1173589200&en=7139707cc4ad6191&ei=5070.

[13] The Lost Tomb of Jesus? Religious Scholar Provides Insight on the Controversy," Science Daily, February 28, 2007. Accessed at http://www.sciencedaily.com/releases/2007/02/070228135009.htm.

[14] "Jesus' Tomb—Pt. 2: Can Christ's Body Be Discovered?" *World News Desk*, March 9, 2007. Accessed at http://www.realtruth.org/news/070309-002-religion.html.

[15] "Beliefs: Trinity, Satan." Accessed at http://www.barna.org/FlexPage.aspx?Page=Topic&TopicID=6.

[16] "Born Again Christians." Accessed at http://www.barna.org/FlexPage.aspx?Page=Topic&TopicID=8.

[17] Gary M. Burge, "The Greatest Story Never Read: Recovering biblical literacy in the church," Christianity Today. Accessed at www.christianitytoday.com/ct/9t9/9t9045.html.

[18] "Jesus' Tomb—Pt. 2: Can Christ's Body Be Discovered?" *World News Desk*, March 9, 2007. Accessed at http://www.realtruth.org/news/070309-002-religion.html.

[19] Simcha Jacobovici and Charles Pellegrino, *The Jesus Family Tomb: the Discovery, the Investigation, and the Evidence That Could Change History*, (San Francisco, CA: Harper San Francisco, 2007), p. vii.

[20] Ibid.

[21] Ibid.

[22] David Horovitz, "Editor's Notes: Giving 'Jesus' the Silent Treatment," *Jerusalem Post*, March 1, 2007. Accessed at http://www.jpost.com/servlet/Satellite?cid=1171894551868&pagename=JPost%2FJPArticle%2FShowFull.

[23] Craig Evans, "The Tomb of Jesus and Family? Second Thoughts." Accessed at http://www.craigaevans.com/tombofjesus.htm.

[24] Karen Matthews, "Documentary Shows Possible Jesus Tomb," *AP News*, February 26, 2007. Accessed at http://news.yahoo.com/s/ap/20070226/ap_on_re_us/jesus_s_burial.

[25] Steve Caruso, "The Lost Tomb of Jesus," *Aramaic Designs*. Accessed at http://www.aramaicdesigns.com/?title=Page:The_Lost_Tomb_of_Jesus.

[26] Ben Witherington, "The Jesus Tomb Show," March 5, 2007. Accessed at http://benwitherington.blogspot.com/.

[27] John J. Miller, "The Fruit of Thy Womb," *National Review*, March 2, 2007. Accessed at http://article.nationalreview.com/?q=NWM4ZWI5N2M2ODc3OGRkNTlhZjUxNWJmNmIoNTNiMjg=&w=MQ==.

[28] "Archaeological Identity Theft: The Lost Tomb of Jesus Fails to Make the Grade," *Extreme Theology*, February 26, 2007. Accessed at http://www.extremetheology.com/.

[29] Ben Witherington, "The Jesus Tomb Show," March 5, 2007. Accessed at http://benwitherington.blogspot.com/.

[30] "Has the Tomb of Jesus Been Found?" CARM Resources. Accessed at http://www.carm.org/evidence/Jesus_tomb.htm.

[31] Cathleen Falsani, "'Titantic' Find or Sacrilege?" *Chicago-Sun Times*, February 27, 2007. Accessed at http://www.suntimes.com/news/falsani/274481,CST-NWS-contro27.article.

[32] Matt Gutman, "Bones of Contention," *ABC News*, February 26, 2007. Accessed at http://abcnews.go.com/Technology/Entertainment/story?id=2905662&page=1.

[33] "Is This Jesus' Tomb?" *People*, March 12, 2007, p. 178.

[34] "Has the Tomb of Jesus Been Found?" CARM Resources. Accessed at http://www.carm.org/evidence/Jesus_tomb.htm.

[35] Ben Witherington, "Problems Multiply for Jesus Tomb Theory," February 28, 2007. Accessed at http://benwitherington.blogspot.com/.

[36] "Archaeological Identity Theft: The Lost Tomb of Jesus Fails to Make the Grade," *Extreme Theology*, February 26, 2007. Accessed at http://www.extremetheology.com/.

[37] Craig Evans, "The Tomb of Jesus and Family? Second Thoughts." Accessed at http://www.craigaevans.com/tombofjesus.htm.

[38] Darrell Bock, "Kloner on DNA and Other Issues," March 10, 2007. Accessed at http://dev.bible.org/bock/node/125.

[39] "The Lost Tomb of Jesus," March 2, 2007. Accessed at http://nasrani.wordpress.com/2007/03/02/the-lost-tomb-of-jesus-the-jesus-family-tomb-discovery-channel-news-analysis/.

[40] Glenna Whitley, "Jesus Junk," *The Dallas Observer*, March 1, 2007. Accessed at http://www.dallasobserver.com/2007-03-01/news/jesus-junk/1.

[41] http://www.prnewswire.com/cgi-bin/stories.pl?ACCT=104&STORY=/www/story/02-25-2007/0004533923&EDATE=

[42] Ben Witherington, "Problems Multiply for Jesus Tomb Theory," February 28, 2007. Accessed at http://benwitherington.blogspot.com/.

[43] Cathleen Falsani, "'Titantic' Find or Sacrilege?" *Chicago-Sun Times*, February 27, 2007. Accessed at http://www.suntimes.com/news/falsani/274481,CST-NWS-contro27.article.

[44] "Nazareth." Accessed at http://en.wikipedia.org/wiki/Nazareth.

[45] Ibid.

[46] "Nazareth," *Walking in their Sandals*. Accessed at http://www.ancientsandals.com/overviews/nazareth.htm.

[47] "Nazareth," Easton's Bible Dictionary. Accessed at http://www.biblegateway.com/resources/dictionaries/dict_meaning.php?source=1&wid=T0002676.

[48] Joe Zias, "The Lost Tomb of Jesus." Accessed at http://www.joezias.com/tomb.html.

[49] Daniel Wallace, "The Lost Tomb of Jesus," March 5, 2007. Accessed at http://www.bible.org/page.php?page_id=4894.

[50] Alan Cooperman, "'Lost Tomb of Jesus' Claim Called A Stunt," *Washington Post*, February 28, 2007. Accessed at http://www.washingtonpost.com/wp-dyn/content/article/2007/02/26/AR2007022600442.html.

[51] "Has the Tomb of Jesus Been Found?" CARM Resources. Accessed at http://www.carm.org/evidence/Jesus_tomb.htm.

[52] Glenna Whitley, "Jesus Junk," *The Dallas Observer*, March 1, 2007. Accessed at http://www.dallasobserver.com/2007-03-01/news/jesus-junk/1.

[53] Simcha Jacobovici and Charles Pellegrino, *The Jesus Family Tomb: the Discovery, the Investigation, and the Evidence That Could Change History*, (San Francisco, CA: Harper San Francisco, 2007), pp. 167-168.

[54] Glenna Whitley, "Jesus Junk," *The Dallas Observer*, March 1, 2007. Accessed at http://www.dallasobserver.com/2007-03-01/news/jesus-junk/1.

[55] Laurie Goodstein," *The New York Times*, February 27, 2007. Accessed at http://www.nytimes.com/2007/02/27/us/27jesus.html?ex=1173589200&en=7139707cc4ad6191&ei=5070.

[56] Ben Witherington, "The Jesus Tomb Show," March 5, 2007. Accessed at http://benwitherington.blogspot.com/.

[57] Michael Easley, John Ankerberg, Dillon Burroughs, *The Da Vinci Code Controversy* (Chicago, IL: Moody, 2006).

[58] Simcha Jacobovici and Charles Pellegrino, *The Jesus Family Tomb: the Discovery, the Investigation, and the Evidence That Could Change History*, (San Francisco, CA: Harper San Francisco, 2007), p. 170.

[59] Ibid, p. 173.

[60] Ibid, p. 174.

[61] "The Lost Tomb of Jesus," *Free Republic*, March 6, 2007. Accessed at http://209.157.64.200/focus/f-religion/1796250/posts.

[62] Nathan Busenitz, "Asking the Experts about Jesus' Lost Tomb," *Pulpit Helps*, March 5, 2007. Accessed at http://www.sfpulpit.com/2007/03/05/asking-the-experts-about-jesus%E2%80%99-lost-tomb/.

[63] "The Jesus Tomb," February 27, 2007. Accessed at http://www.biblicalfoundations.org/?p=92.

[64] A simple online search can prove this, such as the case at http://www.courttv.com/trials/peterson/103003_ctv.html.

[65] Ibid, 142.

⁶⁶ See also chapter nine of Michael Easley, John Ankerberg, and Dillon Burroughs, *The Da Vinci Code Controversy*, (Chicago, IL: Moody, 2006).

⁶⁷ See also Ben Witherington, *What Have They Done With Jesus?*, (San Francisco, CA: Harper San Francisco, 2007), p. 48.

⁶⁸ "Has the Tomb of Jesus Been Found?" CARM Resources. Accessed at http://www.carm.org/evidence/Jesus_tomb.htm.

⁶⁹ "Discerning Fact from Fiction in *The Da Vinci Code*." http://www.evidenceandanswers.com.

⁷⁰ Dan Brown, *The Da Vinci Code*, (New York: Random House, 2003), p. 246.

⁷¹ Hank Hanegraaff and Paul Maier, *The Da Vinci Code: Fact or Fiction* (Downers Grove, IL: Tyndale, 2004), 18.

⁷² Ben Witherington, *The Gospel Code: Novel Claims About Jesus, Mary Magdalene and Da Vinci*. (Downers Grove, IL: Intervarsity Press, 2004) 36.

⁷³ Ibid, 24.

⁷⁴ Darrell Bock, *Breaking The Da Vinci Code* (Nashville, TN: Thomas Nelson, 2004), 23.

⁷⁵ See also, Michael Easley, John Ankerberg, and Dillon Burroughs, *The Da Vinci Code Controversy*, (Chicago, IL: Moody, 2006).

⁷⁶ "What Is the Gospel of Philip?" Accessed at http://www.gotquestions.org/gospel-of-Philip.html.

⁷⁷ Ian Wilson, *Jesus: The Evidence*, (New York: Regnery Publishing, 2000), p. 88.

⁷⁸ Ben Witherington, "Problems Multiply for Jesus Tomb Theory," February 28, 2007. Accessed at http://benwitherington.blogspot.com/.

[79] "Archaeological Identity Theft: The Lost Tomb of Jesus Fails to Make the Grade," *Extreme Theology*, February 26, 2007. Accessed at http://www.extremetheology.com/.

[80] Darrell Bock, "How the Experts Were Used in the Special," March 3, 2007. Accessed at http://dev.bible.org/bock/.

[81] Accessed at http://www.religionnewsblog.com/17587/the-lost-tomb-of-jesus-larry-king-live.

[82] Matti Friedman, "Scholar Offers New Criticism of "Jesus Tomb" Documentary," *AP Worldstream*, March 13, 2007.

[83] Ben Witherington, "The Smoking Gun—Tenth Talpiot Ossuary Proved to Be Blank," March 1, 2007. Accessed at http://benwitherington.blogspot.com/.

[84] Ben Witherington, "The Smoking Gun—Tenth Talpiot Ossuary Proved to Be Blank," March 1, 2007. Accessed at http://benwitherington.blogspot.com/.

[85] "Archaeological Identity Theft: The Lost Tomb of Jesus Fails to Make the Grade," *Extreme Theology*, February 26, 2007. Accessed at http://www.extremetheology.com/.

[86] Daniel Wallace, "The Lost Tomb of Jesus," March 5, 2007. Accessed at http://www.bible.org/page.php?page_id=4894.

[87] Simcha Jacobovici and Charles Pellegrino, *The Jesus Family Tomb: the Discovery, the Investigation, and the Evidence That Could Change History*, (San Francisco, CA: Harper San Francisco, 2007), p. 207.

[88] Robert Kysar in *The Anchor Bible Dictionary*, v. 3, pp. 919-920, cited at http://www.earlychristianwritings.com/john.html.

[89] Simcha Jacobovici and Charles Pellegrino, *The Jesus Family Tomb: the Discovery, the Investigation, and the Evidence That Could Change History*, (San Francisco, CA: Harper San Francisco, 2007), p. 207.

90 Ibid, pp. 207-208.

91 See http://net.bible.org/bible.php?book=Mar&chapter=14#n74.

92 Howard M. Jackson, "The Meaning and Purpose of Mark 14:51-52," *Journal of Biblical Literature*, 116/2 (1997), p. 277.

93 Simcha Jacobovici and Charles Pellegrino, *The Jesus Family Tomb: the Discovery, the Investigation, and the Evidence That Could Change History*, (San Francisco, CA: Harper San Francisco, 2007), p. 208.

94 Ibid, pp. 208-209.

95 Ibid, p. 209.

96 James Tabor, *The Jesus Dynasty*, (New York: Simon & Schuster, 2006), p. 206.

97 Simcha Jacobovici and Charles Pellegrino, *The Jesus Family Tomb: the Discovery, the Investigation, and the Evidence That Could Change History*, (San Francisco, CA: Harper San Francisco, 2007), pp. 105-109.

98 See http://net.bible.org/verse.php?book=john&chapter=11&verse=16.

99 Adapted from Westcott's "Concentric Proofs" as shared by Daniel Wallace, "Introduction to John: Argument, Introduction, and Outline." Accessed at http://www.bible.org/page.php?page_id=1328.

100 Ibid.

101 Jay Tolson, "Who Is Entombed in the 'Jesus Tomb'?", *U.S. News & World Report*, March 12, 2007.

102 "Theological Considerations," Discovery. Accessed at http://dsc.discovery.com/convergence/tomb/theology/theology.html.

103 Cathleen Falsani, "'Titantic' Find or Sacrilege?" *Chicago-Sun Times*, February 27, 2007. Accessed at http://www.suntimes.com/news/falsani/274481,CST-NWS-contro27.article.

[104] Jay Tolson, "Revision for the Greatest Story Ever Told?" *U.S. News & World Report*, February 27, 2007. Accessed at http://www.usnews.com/usnews/news/articles/070227/27jesus_3.htm.

[105] As cited at Albert Mohler, "A.N. Wilson Gets It Too—No Resurrection, No Christianity," March 13, 2007. Accessed at http://www.albertmohler.com/blog.php.

[106] Marc Gellman, "Jesus R.I.P.," *Newsweek*, March 7, 2007. Accessed at http://www.msnbc.msn.com/id/17501882/site/newsweek/page/2/.

[107] Darrell Bock, "Hollywood Hype: The Oscars and Jesus' Family Tomb, What Do They Share?" February, 26, 2007. Accessed at http://dev.bible.org/bock/.

[108] "The Unique Christ" message transcript accessed at http://www.crossroads.ca/unique/un020410.htm.

[109] Michael Foust, "'Jesus Tomb' Documentary Ignores Biblical & Scientific Evidence, Logic, Experts Say," *BP News*, February 27, 2007. Accessed at http://www.bpnews.net/bpnews.asp?ID=25053.

[110] Frederic Kenyon, *The Bible and Archaeology* (New York: Harper & Brothers, 1940), p. 288.

[111] B.F. Westcott, and F.J.A. Hort, eds., *New Testament in Original Greek*, 1881, vol. II, p. 2.

[112] Bruce Metzger, *The Text of the New Testament* (Oxford, Oxford University Press, 1964; revised edition, 1992), p. 34.

[113] Of course, such suggestions are not without critics. For an online discussion, see http://www.preteristarchive.com/Books/1996_thiede_eyewitness.html. The main book on this theory is *Eyewitness to Jesus* by Carsten Peter Thiede and Matthew D'Ancona, (New York: Doubleday, 1996).

[114] Gary Habermas, *The Historical Jesus* (Joplin, MO: College Press, 1996), p. 250.

[115] Josh McDowell, *A Ready Defense*. Accessed at http://www.greatcom.org/resources/areadydefense/.

[116] "Has the Tomb of Jesus Been Found?" CARM Resources. Accessed at http://www.carm.org/evidence/Jesus_tomb.htm.

[117] Matthew Phillips, "Faith Tested," Newsweek, February 28, 2007. Accessed at http://www.msnbc.msn.com/id/17388557/site/newsweek/.

[118] Matthew Phillips, "Faith Tested," Newsweek, February 28, 2007. Accessed at http://www.msnbc.msn.com/id/17388557/site/newsweek/.

[119] Craig Evans, "The Tomb of Jesus and Family? Second Thoughts." Accessed at http://www.craigaevans.com/tombofjesus.htm.

[120] Gary Habermas, "The Lost Tomb of Jesus." Accessed at http://www.garyhabermas.com/articles/The_Lost_Tomb_of_Jesus/losttombofjesus_response.htm.

[121] Matthew Phillips, "Faith Tested," Newsweek, February 28, 2007. Accessed at http://www.msnbc.msn.com/id/17388557/site/newsweek/.

[122] Robert L. Wilken, *The Spirit of Early Christian Thought*, (New Haven, CT: Yale University Press, 2003), p. xv.

[123] Includes adapted material from "The Lost Tomb of Jesus." Accessed at http://en.wikipedia.org/wiki/The_Lost_Tomb_of_Jesus.

[124] Ben Witherington, "The Jesus Tomb Show," March 5, 2007. Accessed at http://benwitherington.blogspot.com/.

[125] Justin Thacker, "These Filmmakers at Peddling Twaddle About Jesus," *The Guardian*, March 1, 2007. Accessed at http://www.guardian.co.uk/religion/Story/0,,2023690,00.html.

[126] John Ankerberg and Dillon Burroughs, *What's the Big Deal About Jesus?* (Eugene, OR: Harvest House, 2007).

[127] See http://dsc.discovery.com/convergence/tomb/explore/media/tomb_evidence.pdf.

[128] Carl Bialik, "Odds of 'Lost Tomb' Being Jesus' Family Rest on Assumptions," *The Wall Street Journal*, March 7, 2007. Accessed at http://online.wsj.com/public/article/SB117338464249431351-ygXzEkoerHU_d3oR6lQUpe2ZhVE_20070407.html?mod=tff_main_tff_top.

[129] Darrell Bock, "Reaction of Tal Ilan and Others," March 4, 2007. Accessed at http://dev.bible.org/bock/.

[130] Mark Goodacre, "The Statistical Case for the Identity of the 'Jesus Family Tomb,'" NT Gateway Blog, March 1, 2007. Accessed at http://ntgateway.com/weblog/2007/03/statistical-case-for-identity-of-jesus.html.

[131] Darrell Bock, "Is Special's Stat Man Backing Off?" March 4, 2007. Accessed at http://dev.bible.org/bock/.

[132] David Horovitz, "Editor's Notes: Giving 'Jesus' the Silent Treatment," *Jerusalem Post*, March 1, 2007. Accessed at http://www.jpost.com/servlet/Satellite?cid=1171894551868&pagename=JPost%2FJPArticle%2FShowFull.

[133] "Has the Tomb of Jesus Been Found?" CARM Resources. Accessed at http://www.carm.org/evidence/Jesus_tomb.htm.

[134] See http://fisher.utstat.toronto.edu/andrey/OfficeHrs.txt.

[135] Daniel Wallace, "The Lost Tomb of Jesus," March 5, 2007. Accessed at http://www.bible.org/page.php?page_id=4894.

[136] Stephen Pfann, "The Improper Application of Statistics in 'The Lost Tomb of Jesus.'" Accessed at http://www.uhl.ac/JudeanTombsAndOssuaries.html.

[137] Ben Witherington, "The Smoking Gun—Tenth Talpiot Ossuary Proved to Be Blank," March 1, 2007. Accessed at http://benwitherington.blogspot.com/.

[138] See http://fisher.utstat.toronto.edu/andrey/OfficeHrs.txt.

[139] "James Ossuary." Accessed at http://en.wikipedia.org/wiki/James_Ossuary.

[140] Ben Witherington, "The Jesus Tomb Show," March 5, 2007. Accessed at http://benwitherington.blogspot.com/.

[141] Ben Witherington, "The Jesus Tomb Show," March 5, 2007. Accessed at http://benwitherington.blogspot.com/.

[142] Simcha Jacobovici and Charles Pellegrino, *The Jesus Family Tomb: the Discovery, the Investigation, and the Efvidence That Could Change History*, (San Francisco, CA: Harper San Francisco, 2007), p. 189.

[143] Ben Witherington, "The Smoking Gun—Tenth Talpiot Ossuary Proved to Be Blank," March 1, 2007. Accessed at http://benwitherington.blogspot.com/.

[144] Ben Witherington, "Problems Multiply for Jesus Tomb Theory," February 28, 2007. Accessed at http://benwitherington.blogspot.com/.

[145] Ben Witherington, "Problems Multiply for Jesus Tomb Theory," February 28, 2007. Accessed at http://benwitherington.blogspot.com/.

[146] John Ankerberg and Dillon Burroughs, "Nine Facts That Disprove the Discovery Channel's The Lost Tomb of Jesus," *ATRI*, March 6, 2007 update. Accessed at http://www.johnankerberg.org/Articles/historical-Jesus/the-Jesus-family-tomb/the-Jesus-family-tomb-9-facts-that-disprove-discovery-channel-lost-tomb-of-jesus.htm.

[147] Ben Witherington, "The Jesus Tomb? Titanic Talpiot Tomb Theory Sunk from the Start," February 26, 2007. Accessed at http://www.johnankerberg.org/Articles/historical-Jesus/the-Jesus-family-tomb/the-Jesus-family-tomb-witherington-response.htm.

[148] Joe Zias, "Viewer's Guide to the Talpiot Tomb." Accessed at http://www.joezias.com/tomb.html.

[149] "Business Connect," *The Columbus Dispatch* (Ohio), March 12, 2007 Monday, p. E1.

[150] R. Thomas Umstead, "'Jesus' Doc Draws 4 Million," *Multichannel News*, March 12, 2007, p. 31.

[151] "'Tomb' with a View," *Daily Variety*, March 7, 2007, p. 5.

[152] "On the Pulse," *Chicago Sun Times*, March 7, 2007, Editorials, p. 37.

[153] "Has the Tomb of Jesus Been Found?" CARM Resources. Accessed at http://www.carm.org/evidence/Jesus_tomb.htm.

[154] Michael Haverluck, "Challenged 'Lost Tomb of Jesus' Airs," *CBN News*, March 4, 2007. Accessed at http://www.cbn.com/cbnnews/112322.aspx.

[155] Matthew Phillips, "Faith Tested," Newsweek, February 28, 2007. Accessed at http://www.msnbc.msn.com/id/17388557/site/newsweek/.

[156] Monica Carter Tagore, "Don't Get Sucked into Latest Claim," *The Shreveport Times*, March 1, 2007. Accessed at http://www.shreveporttimes.com/apps/pbcs.dll/article?AID=/20070228/NEWS0802/702280336/1061/NEWS02.

[157] Adapted from "The Lost Tomb of Jesus." Accessed at http://en.wikipedia.org/wiki/The_Lost_Tomb_of_Jesus.

[158] Karen Matthews, "Documentary Shows Possible Jesus Tomb," *AP News*, February 26, 2007. Accessed at http://news.yahoo.com/s/ap/20070226/ap_on_re_us/jesus_s_burial.

[159] Ibid.

[160] Josh McDowell, "Evidence for the Resurrection." Accessed at http://www.leaderu.com/everystudent/easter/articles/josh2.html.

[161] Cited at the Voice of the Martyrs website, http://www.prisoneralert.com/vompw_persecution.htm.

[162] Craig Evans, in an interview on "A Response to ABC's the Search for Jesus," on *The John Ankerberg Show*, 2001.

[163] Glenna Whitley, "Jesus Junk," *The Dallas Observer*, March 1, 2007. Accessed at http://www.dallasobserver.com/2007-03-01/news/jesus-junk/1.

[164] Whitley, "Jesus Junk," *The Dallas Observer*, March 1, 2007. Accessed at http://www.dallasobserver.com/2007-03-01/news/jesus-junk/1.

[165] Whitley, "Jesus Junk," *The Dallas Observer*, March 1, 2007. Accessed at http://www.dallasobserver.com/2007-03-01/news/jesus-junk/1.

[166] http://www.cnn.com/2007/TECH/science/02/26/jesus.sburial.ap/index.html.

[167] From Joel Rosenberg, "New Film Claims Jesus Didn't Rise from the Dead, Body Has Been Found," February 25, 2007. Accessed at http://joelrosenberg.blogspot.com/.

[168] "Laurie Goodstein," *The New York Times*, February 27, 2007. Accessed at http://www.nytimes.com/2007/02/27/us/27jesus.html?ex=1173589200&en=7139707cc4ad6191&ei=5070.

[169] "Laurie Goodstein," *The New York Times*, February 27, 2007. Accessed at http://www.nytimes.com/2007/02/27/us/27jesus.html?ex=1173589200&en=7139707cc4ad6191&ei=5070.

170 This article was originally posted at www.johnankerberg.org where the Lost Tomb of Jesus resource section received over 6,500 hits in just the first few days. A special thanks to the Ankerberg Theological Research Institute and Dr. John Ankerberg for allowing me to reprint this article here for maximum impact.

171 Darrell Bock, "Hollywood Hype: The Oscars and Jesus' Family Tomb, What Do They Share?" February, 26, 2007. Accessed at http://dev.bible.org/bock/.

172 From Joel Rosenberg, "New Film Claims Jesus Didn't Rise from the Dead, Body Has Been Found," February 25, 2007. Accessed at http://joelrosenberg.blogspot.com/.

173 Ibid.

174 Darrell Bock, "Is Special's Stat Man Backing Off?" March 4, 2007. Accessed at http://dev.bible.org/bock/.

175 Ibid.

176 Darrell Bock, "Reaction of Tal Ilan and Others," March 4, 2007. Accessed at http://dev.bible.org/bock/.

177 Ben Witherington, "The Jesus Tomb? Titanic Talpiot Tomb Theory Sunk from the Start," February 26, 2007. Accessed at http://www.johnankerberg.org/Articles/historical-Jesus/the-Jesus-family-tomb/the-Jesus-family-tomb-witherington-response.htm.

178 Michael Easley, John Ankerberg, Dillon Burroughs, *The Da Vinci Code Controversy* (Chicago, IL: Moody, 2006).

179 Darrell Bock, "How the Experts Were Used in the Special," March 3, 2007. Accessed at http://dev.bible.org/bock/.

180 Ben Witherington, "The Jesus Tomb? Titanic Talpiot Tomb Theory Sunk from the Start," February 26, 2007. Accessed at

http://www.johnankerberg.org/Articles/historical-Jesus/the-Jesus-family-tomb/the-Jesus-family-tomb-witherington-response.htm.

[181] Karen Matthews, "Documentary Shows Possible Jesus Tomb," *AP News*, February 26, 2007. Accessed at http://news.yahoo.com/s/ap/20070226/ap_on_re_us/jesus_s_burial.

[182] Ibid.

[183] Darrell Bock, "Hollywood Hype: The Oscars and Jesus' Family Tomb, What Do They Share?" February, 26, 2007. Accessed at http://dev.bible.org/bock/.

[184] Dr. William Lane Craig in M. Wilkins and J.P. Moreland, editors, *Jesus Under Fire* (Grand Rapids, MI: Zondervan, 1995), p. 149.

[185] Paul Althaus in Wolfhart Pannenberg, *Jesus-God and Man* (SCM Press, 1968), p. 100.

[186] "Are Christians Intolerant to Claim Jesus Is the Only Way?" on *The John Ankerberg Show*, 2001.

[187] "Are Christians Intolerant to Claim Jesus Is the Only Way?" on *The John Ankerberg Show*, 2001.

[188] "The Disciples Stole Jesus' Body and Faked His Resurrection," *CARM Resources*. Accessed at http://www.carm.org/evidence/fakedresurrection.htm.

[189] Matthew 28:11-15.

About the Author

Author and speaker Dillon Burroughs has appeared in numerous locations nationwide and abroad. On subjects related to comparative religions and Christianity and culture, Dillon's written works have appeared on James Dobson's Focus on the Family, *The New York Times*, *The Washington Post*, Salem Radio Network news, Moody Radio Network, *iLife* Television Network, Prime Time America, *Leadership Journal*, NBC affiliates, The John Ankerberg Show, *Discipleship Journal, Group Magazine*, and many other media outlets.

Dillon's books include the **#1 Amazon bestselling e-book**, *The Use of the Bible in The Da Vinci Code*, the books *The Da Vinci Code Controversy, Get in the Game, Misquotes in Misquoting Jesus, The Cults and Christianity, World Religions and Christianity,* and *Middle East Meltdown*. In addition, Dillon has edited projects with several of today's top Christian personalities, including Dr. Tim LaHaye (co-creator of the *Left Behind* series), Dr. Tony Evans (President, The Urban Alternative), Dr. John MacArthur (President, The Master's College & Seminary), Dr. John Ankerberg (Host, The John Ankerberg Show), Dr. Michael Easley (President, Moody Bible Institute), and Dr. Gary Chapman (author of the NY Times bestseller *The Five Love Languages* and *The Five Languages of Apology*). In total, Dillon's written works have sold over 28,000 copies in his first year (*The Da Vinci Code Controversy, Get in the Game, Misquotes in Misquoting Jesus, Middle East Meltdown*), while his edited projects have sold over 2 million copies combined, including the best-sellers, *The Five Apology Languages* and *The Five Love Languages* series. Dillon has also served as a regular contributor for *Group Magazine*, America's most-read youth ministry resource.

As a communicator, Dillon has shared the platform with several diverse personalities, ranging from Texas senator Kay Bailey Hutchinson, former Dallas Seminary president Dr. John Walvoord, and actress Susan Colon ("The Young and the Restless," "Family Matters") to musical artists such as Seven Day Slumber, Michael Tait (of DC Talk), Petra, and Rachel Lampa.

Over the past decade, he has spoken to 35,000 people in churches, schools, juvenile centers, concerts, and missionary contexts.

Dillon Burroughs is a ThM graduate from Dallas Theological Seminary in addition to graduating with a B.S. degree in Communications from Indiana State University. He lives in the Indianapolis, Indiana area with his wife, Deborah, and children, Ben and Natalie.

Publisher Information

AMAZON UPGRADE

If you purchased this book from Amazon.com, you can acquire online access via Amazon Upgrade.

ORDERING THIS BOOK IN QUANTITY

Nimble Books does not provide direct fulfillment of individual bookseller or distributor orders. All orders should be placed through our wholesaler, Ingram.

If you are interested in purchasing in quantity (2 or more), we will drop ship for 27.5% discount off list; you pay shipping and handling.

ABOUT NIMBLE BOOKS

Our trusty Merriam-Webster Collegiate Dictionary defines "nimble" as follows:

> 1: quick and light in motion: AGILE *nimble fingers*
>
> 2 a: marked by quick, alert, clever conception, comprehension, or resourcefulness *a nimble mind* b: RESPONSIVE, SENSITIVE *a nimble listener*

And traces the etymology to the 14th Century:

> Middle English nimel, from Old English numol holding much, from niman to take; akin to Old High German neman to take, Greek nemein to distribute, manage, nomos pasture, nomos usage, custom, law

The etymology is reminiscent of the old Biblical adage, "to whom much is given, much is expected" (Luke 12:48). Nimble Books seeks to honor that Christian principle by combining the spirit of *nimbleness* with the Biblical concept of *abundance:* we deliver what you need to know about a subject in a quick, resourceful, and sensitive manner.

NIMBLE BOOKS LLC

Colophon

This book was produced using Microsoft Word and Adobe Acrobat. The cover was produced using The Gimp 2.0.2 with Ghostscript. The cover font is Constantia The spine is Verdana.

Heading fonts and the body text inside the book are in Constantia, chosen because it is a nimble-looking font that is new enough to be fresh on the eyes. Quotations are in Trebuchet MS, a font whose name has nicely medieval connotations.

The American Heritage® Dictionary of the English Language, Fourth Edition, copyright © 2000 by Houghton Mifflin Company defines col·o·phon as follows:

> An ancient Greek city of Asia Minor northwest of Ephesus. It was famous for its cavalry.

Along the same lines, Webster's Revised Unabridged, copyright 1996, 1998, MICRA, Inc.:

> \Col"o*phon\ (k[o^]l"[-o]*f[o^]n), n. [L. colophon finishing stroke, Gr. kolofw`n; cf. L. culmen top, collis hill. Cf. Holm.] An inscription, monogram, or cipher, containing the place and date of publication, printer's name, etc., formerly placed on the last page of a book.

The colophon, then, represents the summit, or fulfillment, of an act of creation. According to Christian theology the meaning and purpose of the empty tomb and the risen Jesus was the creation (and recreation) of a world where sinners are restored to grace.

Fred Zimmerman

Publisher, Nimble Books LLC

www.ingramcontent.com/pod-product-compliance
Lightning Source LLC
Chambersburg PA
CBHW070552170426
43201CB00012B/1811